CONTEMPORARY STAGE ROLES FOR WOMEN

CONTEMPORARY STAGE ROLES FOR WOMEN

A Descriptive Catalogue

Compiled by
SANDRA HEYS

Greenwood Press
Westport, Connecticut • London, England

Library of Congress Cataloging in Publication Data

Heys, Sandra.
  Contemporary stage roles for women.

  Bibliography: p.
  Includes indexes.
    1. Women—Drama—Indexes.   2. American drama—20th
century—Indexes.   3. English drama—20th century—
Indexes.   4. Sex role in literature.   5. Actresses.
6. Acting.   I. Title.
PN2054.H49   1985   822 '.91 '0809287   84-19218
ISBN 0-313-24473-1 (lib. bdg.)

Library of Congress Catalog Card Number: 84-19218
ISBN: 0-313-24473-1

First published in 1985

Greenwood Press
A division of Congressional Information Service, Inc.
88 Post Road West, Westport, Connecticut 06881
Printed in the United States of America

10 9 8 7 6 5 4 3 2 1

To Bob,

who was behind me every step of the way, who not only gave encouragement
and immeasurable emotional support, but also the use of his word processor

Contents

Acknowledgments

A number of people gave assistance, guidance, information, and support to this effort by either making suggestions of plays that had interesting roles for women or by giving technical advice on the many steps involved in writing this book. Thanks to Rob Harden, Jean Bryant, Julie Hunger, Kit Ellis, Gloria Albee, Pearl Castle, Elizabeth Bray, Larry Fletcher, Florence Fieler, Ruth Cohen, Lynn Loacker and the Pacific Northwest Writers Conference.

Introduction

THE PROBLEM AND THE SOLUTION

Women drawn to perform in the theater have been handicapped for centuries. In Shakespeare's time, women were not even allowed on the stage. In the 19th century, women well established in the theater resorted to playing male roles for want of interesting female roles. Lack of rewarding roles remains a problem today. The typical part available is as somebody's sweetheart, somebody's wife, somebody's mother, or a prostitute; the female being defined in terms of a major male character. Opportunities for a woman to play a central character are rare.

Liberalized attitudes about women have been reflected recently in television and film scripts and a renaissance is beginning with women increasing their authority in all walks of life. But the stage repertory, being a collection of plays written over a long period of time, lags behind. Good material for the stage is being written but is slow to reach the public. The goal of this work is to spotlight published, accessible plays with strong female roles, expose these valuable resources to performers, and, through increased use, encourage publication of more plays that meet the needs of women.

Female Stereotypes

The tools of a musician are her instrument and the repertoire written for that instrument. If, for instance, her instrument is the flute, she will have as the tools of her trade her instrument and all the music that has been written for it. If a woman chooses acting as her form of expression, the tools of her trade are her body, voice, face, and the dramatic roles that have been written for women.

When a woman begins her search for roles to play, she will find, first, that there are half as many female parts as male parts from which to choose. Second, most of the roles she finds will be negative cultural stereotypes:

* victim/wimp

* prostitute/floozy

* neurotic

* trivialized, nagging wife/mother-in-law

* "second banana" (a vaudeville term for the second-ranked
   comedian: the top banana had all the laugh lines; the
   second banana was there to give cues and set up the
   jokes)

* one dimensional (e.g., while male roles are well-delineated
   the female role may be described merely as "the girl")

This kind of role provides little satisfaction for the
performer and is enough to discourage the most persistent, determined aspirant. Ironically, a large proportion of aspirants to a
theatrical career are female. Thus, acting classes are often
predominantly female, while the opportunities available in terms
of material are limited and the environment stifling. Teachers of
acting classes have difficulty providing material with enough
variety and scope to challenge their female students and stretch
their abilities. The few substantial scenes employing women get
worn out from overuse.

The price women have paid to win and maintain a theatrical
career often has been to play compromising and degrading roles.
Many very talented women leave their theatrical dreams behind
each year for this reason. While a professional who expects this
work to be her livelihood may need to adopt the philosophy "the
one who pays the fiddler calls the tune," the large number of
female performers in community and school groups need not feel
this constraint. They have a greater measure of freedom in the
selection of performance material.

True, there are elements of the stereotypes listed above
that are a part of women's experience, and some plays included
below show this side of it. Women's history is filled with
frustration, subjugation, misery, and grief. A goal of this book
is to stop this self-perpetuating cycle and take off in a new direction to foster positive images of women on stage.

Creating Positive Images

Theater is a ritual about life experiences. Rather than
continuing to ritualize the negative aspects of women's history,
why not create a positive celebration of powerful, competent,
successful, and loving women? Theater is a mirror of life, but
life may also mirror the theater. Our understanding of who we are
comes from the mental images we have of ourselves and from the
role models we have experienced. Characters in the theater can
be very real role models. Young people, forming their own impres-
sions of the world, are especially susceptible. If one believes

that a change of attitudes about women is necessary, then con-
tinued repetition of undesirable attitudes will work against us
as such attitudes become more deeply ingrained in our consciousness.
     The traditional symbol of theater, the two masks laughing
and crying, sets the tone for this collection. I have strived to
maintain a balance by including at least as many positive images
as negative ones, from a field where the negative dominates.
The plays were chosen to appeal to a wide range of tastes and
preferences to give the greatest measure of choice to the reader.

The Contemporary Character

     A contemporary character may be defined as a person who has
emerged or is emerging from the old mold of being subordinate to
all male figures. Traditionally, woman's primary purpose was to
serve others. In the new era, serving others will be based on
personal preference rather than on gender. Traditionally, a woman's identity was based on the males in her family; in the future
it will be based upon who she is and what she does. While there
is nothing inherently right or wrong with a person choosing to be
passive, such a person often tends to be less interesting on the
stage.
     The contemporary character takes matters into her own hands
and acts rather than is acted upon. Thus, some women from the
past, such as Elizabeth I from the 16th century and Major Barbara
from the early 20th century, will fit this definition of contemporary, while other women living closer to the present will not.
If our contemporary character is a tragic figure, it might be
because her individuality is in conflict with the system.   Like
the classical tragic figure, she has an air of nobility about
her.   But, more often than not, she triumphs because the early
20th century belief that the individual is at the mercy of the
system is giving way to a new philosophy of optimism and re-
emergence of the individual.

SELECTING AND DELINEATING ROLES

It is essential that women be on the decision-making levels of production to bring their awareness of the full range of woman's experience to the process of choosing plays for production and delineating female characters. It is hoped that men, too, will have this sensitivity if, as playwrights, producers, or directors, they are in a position to create or define female roles. After all, the play will be presented to an increasingly aware audience.

Women performers already well established in theater and film name their terms and make their own decisions about which characters they will portray. Helen Mirren, in the film Long Good Friday, agreed to take the role of a gun moll only after the part had been rewritten to give the character more gumption and dimension. Jane Fonda or Barbara Streisand is in a position to buy the rights to a script having a role she would like to play and then producing it herself. Women in community and school theater also have this power to determine roles; they need but exercise it.

Being well-versed and aware of theater literature will provide the necessary ammunition for a woman seeking to influence or determine role choice. The information that this guide presents can help put women in a decision-making posture rather than in the passive position of gratefully accepting whichever roles are offered. A positive corollary of selecting strong roles for women lies in supporting those writers who are creating such material.

Revising Scripts

One of the realities of writing for the theater is that the playwright's words are subject to change by many people connected with the production. Plays headed for a New York opening are rewritten and revised continually during rehearsal and out-of-town tryouts, and the play that opens can be completely different from the original script. Theater is a collaborative effort, and everybody gets his or her two cents in before the plays opens.

There is no reason why a woman should obediently accept a part just as it is written. If she is bored with playing weak, inept, and colorless characters, she can breathe life into some of these roles. When it is not essential to the action of the play that the female character be a wimp, her character can be strengthened and her part can be salvaged. If the offensive character is inherent to the theme of the play, the performer has the option to reject the part, while the producer has the option to find another play.

Ways to Improve a Role

* Delete remarks made by the character which unnecessarily cast her into a negative stereotype. What a person says and how she says it gives us much information about her.

* Delete offensive remarks made to the character. Here is an opportunity to right some wrongs. Any statement that seems patronizing, condescending, or degrading may be taken out. An example of this is the scene in Finishing Touches between Katy and her husband, Jeff. Jeff is in love with another woman, and his unhappiness with his marriage relationship expresses itself in many ways. He makes a series of derogatory remarks to Katy about her being disorderly and criticizes her bathrobe. These can be removed and Katy will come out in a stronger, more positive light.

* Delete derogatory descriptions of the character made by other characters. What is said by others is a major source of information about her. An example of how this operates in a positive manner occurs in Favourite Nights where the leading character, Catherine is established largely by the other characters in the play: her sister, her father, and her students, who profusely praise her accomplishments. We know she is brilliant because the others say she is.

* Delete offensive actions involving the character. An example can be found in the scene from The Miracle Worker where Annie, newly arrived at the Keller household, is locked in her room by Helen. She is humiliated by having the entire family find out and has to come out through the window and then down a ladder. We get the message that she has been humiliated, but to have Captain Keller carry Annie down the ladder on his shoulders is going too far. Annie can descend the ladder on her own without compromising her character delineation. This kind of thinking can be applied to a variety of situations.

A word of warning: Occasionally a playwright stipulates that not a word of the script may be changed without the author's permission. This notice will appear prominently at the beginning of the script with information about the production rights.

It might often be difficult to separate the stereotyped material from the character as it appears to be inextricably interwoven into her personality, but we need to start thinking in those terms. What would Carole in Blank Pages be like if she weren't self-deprecating? What other aspects of her personality are interesting? A character worth portraying on the stage will have many interesting facets to her personality.

Those characteristics that fall into the syndrome defined as female stereotypes are not, in reality, exclusive to women. Men also have these patterns and it is not suggested that we limit expression of the full range of human experience for women by systematically closing off the expression of one aspect of it. But, the expectation that any female person will automatically fit the stereotyped mold needs to change. The most effective way to eliminate a stereotype is to counter it with the opposite condition. Black people used the motto "black is beautiful" to change their image, and we now find many black characters in television series who are competent, wise, and assertive. Women need to find a positive focus in order to see themselves as effective, powerful beings and to eliminate their stereotypes.

Redesigning Male Roles

   Roles originally written for men provide a rich source of material. An example is the play Whose Life Is It Anyway?, the story of a paralyzed man wishing to die but being kept alive by life-support machines. Mary Tyler Moore played the lead in the New York production. In a remake of It's a Wonderful Life, Marlo Thomas played the role originally portrayed by Jimmy Stewart, while Cloris Leachman took the role of the formerly male angel. Joan Rivers and Nancy Walker played the leads in a production of The Odd Couple.
   The only time it is absolutely required that a man play the role is in an instance where the masculinity of the character is inherent to the action of the play: when the character is some-one's father, husband, brother; or some other specified male relation (and that hasn't stopped some women in the past from taking such roles). In fact, why couldn't the brother be changed to a sister? The plays Dentist and Patient by William Saroyan and The Eye of the Beholder by Kent Broadhurst are included in the listings as examples of how this can be done. The family relationships of the dentist and the patient are not part of the story. The characters in Eye of the Beholder are two artists and their model working in a studio, so they could be either gender. Narrators have almost always been male yet there is no reason why they could not be female as well.
   The same reasoning applies to women in minority groups who have been stereotyped and excluded in our culture. In the classi-fied listing of roles following the main play listings below, a selection of roles that have been specifically written for minor-ity women can be found. Beyond that, however, a large proportion of roles originally designed for white characters can be played by minority members. Friends or associates of characters can easily be of different ethnic backgrounds without affecting the reality level of the production. Some schools and community theaters have made the decision to ignore completely the racial characteristics of their players in casting parts, and even have racially mixed families in their productions.

USING THE CATALOGUE

Subscribing to the philosophy of the show-biz old timer who said, "The only bad publicity is an obituary," my first criterion in choosing each play is that women get a big piece of the action.   The second standard is that the play be dramatically sound and play well on the stage.   The third measure is that the role does not reinforce negative female stereotypes.   Plays blatantly offensive are happily omitted.   Some works, however, are not clearly black or white, but fall into a gray area where the offensiveness is questionable. As individual responses to sexism vary, if there are strong indications of merit in other respects the play is listed.

Despite the aforementioned high ideals, what we have to work with is the body of dramatic literature as it exists today, which reflects all the prejudices and biases of the culture at large; so the roles in many cases are far from being all we'd like them to be. Stereotypes are difficult to eliminate and insidiously persist despite our efforts. Thus, the selections are the best of what is available at the present. The pervasive nature of stereotypes is such that very few works manage to avoid them completely.   This would be a very short catalogue if absolute standards were applied.

On the positive side, a myriad of subtleties in how the performer carries out her part will affect how stereotyped the final rendition of the role will be. An enlightened performance can do a lot to lessen or eliminate a negative stereotype in a character. Bessie and Flora in A Perfect Analysis for a Parrot could be played in a stereotyped manner, or they could be broadly comic, or the pathos could be emphasized. Of course, the use of the word "girl" to describe women in this play would be edited out. Such stopgap measures may not be needed for long, as the trend is rapidly moving in the direction of improved quality of material for women performers.

Finding Scripts

The scripts included were chosen for their availability. Most of them can be found in local libraries or ordered through a library.   The name of the agent or publisher who controls the rights to a play is provided with the play listing, and these addresses are compiled in an appendix directory.

Parts of the Book and Terminology

The alphabetical listing of "Plays and Female Roles" briefly describes each play and characterizes the female roles, in order of importance. Because the lengths of plays vary, the actual lengths of the parts will vary. The following terms will be used to describe the length of the parts listed.

1. [LEAD]: the character is central to the plot and has a substantial portion of the action.

2. [SUPPORTING ROLE]: a secondary character; a part of medium length.

3. [SHORT ROLE]: incidental character; shorter role.

4. [BIT PART]: a character with a very short appearance.

Playwrights and dates are given along with publishers or agents. The abbreviation "Dram. Pl. Ser." signifies Dramatists Play Service, and the number after the Best Short Plays series notation is the year of publication. With each listing is a numerical count of women's and men's roles (e.g., "3w 2m"), and an appendix classifies plays according to gender distribution. Plays with all female casts and those with mixed casts are each ranked according to number of female roles. Where the casting calls for children, the play listing includes a notation of the age requirements. Once past adolescence (around 14 or 15 for females or at the point where the character could be played by an adult), the characters are included in the stated number of women's roles.

A special feature of this volume is the classification of roles following the main play listing. Roles are listed by play and catalogued according to age groupings (20s and younger, 30-40, 40-50, 50-60, 60s and over); character types (heroic, kind and nurturing, comic, villainous, tragic, unique, high brow, low brow, disturbed); unusual physical characteristics (overweight, oversized, hearing or visually impaired, wheelchair bound); and roles for specific minorities (Asian, Black, Hispanic).

Names of characters and playwrights may be traced through specific indexes included in the backmatter. In addition, a bibliography lists selected anthologies of plays by, for, and about women, works about women in theater, women in literature, and relevant general sources.

Audience Suitability Rating

Some means was thought necessary to communicate the broad range of audience acceptability found in the plays listed akin to the rating system used by the film industry, which labels a film G, PG, R, or X. Most of the plays listed here would be acceptable to a general adult or young adult audience with little or no editing. Plays that might get an "R" or an " X" rating by the film industry will have some annotation indicating elements that might be objectionable in certain circumstances. Examples include extreme profanity, sexually explicit actions, sexually explicit language, and violence.

Building a Repertoire

This work is intended to be a tool for repertoire building on two levels. First, on the individual level, a performer develops a selection of pieces that she is prepared to perform; and second, on the broader level, women as a group have a body of literature available to them as performers.

Some thought and effort will be needed to cultivate and maintain a repertoire for women. One must be alert for new scripts as they become available, and keep informed of trends. One must be a collector of script titles and notations on roles in order to create the best possible opportunities for women performers. When attention is focused on this goal, more material will appear. Keeping this data together in a systematic way will make it more accessible and useful, and when the need for new material arises, it will be available.

There is bound to be good material that was missed in this work and new plays with potentially strong roles are coming out each year. It is suggested that whenever an attractive role comes to a reader's attention, she make note of it and share and compare notes with other women performers. The author, too, would welcome such comments sent to her in care of the publisher.

As with the above definition of contemporary characters, contemporary women interested in theatrical careers must take action and do whatever can be done to develop material rather than wait for someone else to provide it, for, given past experience, it might be a long wait. There is much that a performer can do by her own power to improve her opportunities, thereby letting actors, producers, and playwrights know that women have a new set of expectations. Theater is a powerful arena for challenging beliefs, thoughts, and attitudes. While in the past it has been instrumental in the denigration of women, that can be turned around quickly, decisively, and thoroughly if women desire it and take the necessary actions to accomplish it.

CONTEMPORARY STAGE ROLES FOR WOMEN

PLAYS AND FEMALE ROLES

ABSENT FRIENDS, Allan Ayckbourn (1974)   Samuel French
3w 3m

Conflict arises among affluent friends over an extra-marital affair involving members of their set. British.

> Diana: late 30s, [lead], tense, suspicious, worrisome.
> Evelyn: late 20s-early 30s, [supporting role], stylish and trendy.
> Marge: 30s, [supporting role], enjoys fussing over sick husband.

ABSURD PERSON SINGULAR, Allan Ayckbourn (1974)   Samuel French
3w 3m

The Christmas get-togethers of three couples (an employer and two men who work for him) over a three-year period show the changes going on in their lives. British.

> Jane: 30s, [supporting role], compulsively neat homemaker.
> Marion: early 40s, [supporting role], had drinking problem, the wife of the boss.
> Eve: 30s, [supporting role], on tranquilizers, makes several comic suicide attempts.

AGNES OF GOD, John Pielmeier (1978)   Andrew Gellis
3w

A psychiatrist attempts to solve the mystery of a nun with strange powers, who remembers nothing of her newborn baby found dead.

> Dr. Martha Livingstone: 50s, [lead], psychiatrist, rational scientist, bitter former Catholic.

Mother Miriam Ruth: 30-50s, [lead], mystical nun, defends
the church, tries to protect Agnes.
Agnes: teens-early 20s, [lead], innocent nun, sheltered,
doesn't know where babies come from, has miraculous powers.

AN ALMOST PERFECT PERSON, Judith Ross (1977)   Samuel French
1w 2m

At the close of a busy political campaign for a congressional
seat, a woman takes time out for two romantic affairs.

Irene Porter: early 40s, [lead], vital, vibrant, warm, intelligent, witty, strong convictions, idealistic, mother,
widow, attorney.

AM I BLUE?, Beth Henley (1972)   Dram. Pl. Ser.
4w 3m

A shy, awkward, 17-year-old man sent to a brothel by his frater-
nity brothers is rescued by a street wise 16-year-old woman.
Short play.

Ashbe: 16, [lead], neglected, self reliant, cheerful, un-
happy family life yet able to find beauty and happiness
in unexpected corners.
Hilda: 35, [short role], curt, outspoken, coarse, waitress.
Clareece: 14-15, [bit part], teeny bopper.
Prostitute: [bit part], non speaking.

THE AMERICAN DREAM, Edward Albee (1961)   Dram. Pl. Ser.
3w 2m

Sharp-edged portrayal of a troubled American family. Short play.

Mommy: 40s [lead], bossy, cruel.
Grandma: 86, [lead], feisty, crafty, nasty.
Mrs. Baker: 40s, [supporting role], arrogant club chair-
person, busy committee member.

AND, Robert Gordon (1974)   West Coast Plays #2
1w 1m(non speaking)

Frightening monologue by a woman talking to the body of her husband whom she has just murdered. Short play.

Ruth: 50s, [lead], tired, drawn, much repressed anger and
resentment, tidy and well-behaved on the surface.

AND IF THAT MOCKINGBIRD DON'T SING, William Whitehead (1977)
Flora Roberts or West Coast Plays #3
2w 13m

Her truck stop cafe in New Mexico is losing business, but Casey is living in happier past memories when she and her deceased husband were country western singing stars. Black role.

> Casey: late 30s, [lead], slightly tired, but resolute, un-daunted, warm, generous, had very happy marriage before her husband died, sings several songs.
> Darlene: 50s, [supporting role], black, waitress, tough, kind, loyal to Casey, outspoken, coarse.

AND MISS REARDON DRINKS A LITTLE, Paul Zindel (1971)
Dram. Pl. Ser.
5w 2m

Three sisters, professional educators, struggling with their personal problems are forced to face reality with powerful impact when the couple living downstairs from them intrudes.

> Catherine: 40s [lead], oldest sister, assistant principal, judgmental, argumentative, has drinking problem.
> Ceil Adams: 40s, [lead], middle sister, very successful school administrator, married the man her sister loved.
> Anna Reardon: 40s, [lead], youngest sister, teacher, ob-sessed with death, having an emotional breakdown.
> Fleur Steen: 40s [supporting role] tense, trite teacher.
> Mrs. Pentrano: anywhere over 35, [short role], comic, build-ing manager, sells cosmetics, not-too-bright, malaprop.

THE AU PAIR MAN, Hugh Leonard (1968)   Samuel French
1w 1m

A grand, older, English woman takes in a rough Irish workingman to do chores and agrees to teach him how to be a gentleman.

> Mrs. Rogers: 40s-early 50s, [lead], stately, educated, ac-complished, well-to-do, very British.

AUGUSTUS, Jean Anouilh, Jean Aurenche (1969) Best Short Plays 69
2w 3m (extras)

A young Duke able to speak only one word each day due to a strange affliction vainly tries to proclaim his love to a woman. Short play.

> Duchess: 50-70s, (action of play spans ten years or more) [lead], matriarch, grandmother, of Duke, imposing, ele-gant, proud, grand.

Helene: teens-25, [short role], object of Duke's love, rides
bicycle, smiles tenderly, gentle, polite, hard-of-hearing.

AUNTIE MAME, Jerome Lawrence, Robert E. Lee (1957) Dram. Pl. Ser.
12w 28m

Ten-year-old Patrick is sent to live with his zany libertine aunt
in New York City in 1928 and finds his life dramatically changed.
Comedy.

Auntie Mame: 30s through 40s, (action spans 9 years) [lead],
courageous, adventurous, sparkling, spirited, progressive
thinker, ultra sophisticate.
Vera: 30-40s, [supporting role], comic friend of Mame, stage
star, puts on airs, heavy drinker.
Norah Muldoon: 20-40s [short role], spunky nanny who cares
for Patrick.
Sally Cato MacDougal: 20-30s [short role], gorgeous, South-
ern belle.
Mother Burnside: 60-70s, [short role], mother-in-law, in
wheelchair, formidable.
Agnes Gooch: 20-30s, [short role], comic, plain secretary
who transforms into a glamorous, sexy woman.
Gloria Upson: early 20s, [supporting role], snobbish fiancee
of Patrick, narrow minded, trite, bland.
Doris Upson: 40-50s, [supporting role], Gloria's mother,
shallow, narrow minded, suburbanite.
Pegeen Ryan: 20-30s, [short role].
Cousin Fan: [short role].
Maid: [short role].
Customer: [short role].

THE AUTOGRAPH HOUND, James Prideaux (1968)   Dram. Pl. Ser.
2w 1m

Lila goes through fantastic machinations to collect celebrity au-
tographs letting her family relationships suffer. Short play.

Lila: late 40s, [lead], short, plump, frumpy, energetic, tyrannical.
Cissie: 19, [supporting role], Lila's daughter, plain, awkward, ill-fitting clothes, lethargic.

THE AUTUMN GARDEN, Lillian Hellman (1952)   Dram. Pl. Ser.
7w 5m

In 1949 at a gulf resort near New Orleans, a group of unhappy
people come to grips with the futility of their lives.

Rose Griggs: 40s, [lead], formerly pretty, soft looking,
flirtatious, in loveless marriage.

Constance Tuckerman: 40s, [lead], dignified, prim, hostess
    and owner of summer house, romantic illusions, sacrificed
    her life for an unobtainable love.
Nina: 40s, [lead], attractive, chic, tired, delicate, self
    contempt, pretends to be understanding and forgiving
    wife.
Carrie Ellis: 40s, [supporting role], distinguished looking.
Mary Ellis: 70s, [supporting role], sometimes sprightly,
    other times senile.
Sophie Tuckerman: 17, [supporting role], over polite, shy,
    war refugee, manages to escape unhappiness of others.
Maid: [short role], German speaking.

A BAD YEAR FOR TOMATOES, John Patrick (1973)   Dram. Pl. Ser.
4w 3m

A busy television performer, tired of her career, seeks quiet and
solitude in a small New England town only to become involved with
some frivolous neighbors and a trifling murder mystery.

Myra Marlowe: 40-50s, [lead], witty, fed up with the enter-
    tainment business, wishes to grow tomatoes and write her
    autobiography.
Cora Gump: 40-60s, [supporting role], small town, friendly,
    well meaning, trite.
Reba Harper: 40-60s, [supporting role], small town gossip,
    conventional, provincial.
Willa Mae Wilcox: 40-60s [supporting role], small, furtive,
    suspected witch, interested in the occult.

BAG LADY, Jean-Claude van Itallie (1980)   Dram. Pl. Ser.
1w

Big city life as seen from the viewpoint of a roving collector of
other people's discards. Short play.

Clara: 50s, [lead], shabbily dressed, wears big overcoat,
    mutters to herself, carries several bags.

THE BATHTUB, Lisa Shipley (1979)   West Coast Plays #5
2w

A woman retreating from the world by staying in the bathtub for
two weeks is finally persuaded by her roommate/lover to emerge.
Short play.

Joyce: 20s, [lead], artistic, intelligent, neurotic, in-
    fantile.
Leann: 20s, [supporting role], Joyce's roommate, patient,
    the more reasonable of the pair.

BEAUTY AND THE BEAST, Frank Marcus (1975)

Plays of the Year vol. 46

6w 4m

This updated version of an old fairy tale is laced with humor and modern perspective.

> Mrs. C. Crunch: 823 yrs. old, [lead], "a good old English witch", gruff, practical, comic.
> Madame Suzanne: several hundred years old, [supporting role], "fairly good French fairy", strong French accent, rouged, extravagant mannerisms.
> Beauty: 16, [lead], youngest daughter of merchant, lovely, kind, tender hearted, generous, optimistic, hard worker, loves animals.
> Hyacinth: 18, [supporting role], spoiled, self centered, ill-tempered, lazy, greedy, frivolous, second daughter of merchant.
> Petunia: 20, [supporting role], spoiled, self centered, ill-tempered, lazy, greedy, eldest daughter.
> Mary Jane: 12, [short role], listener for Mrs. Crunch's story.

BEDROOM FARCE, Allan Ayckbourn (1975)   Samuel French

4w 4m

The quarrels between Susannah and Trevor cause disruption in the lives of three couples among their friends and relatives. Comedy.

> Delia: 50s, [supporting role], mother of Trevor, cranky, complaining.
> Susannah: 20-30s, [supporting role], in an emotional crisis in her relationship with her husband, Trevor, throwing tantrums, frightened, nervous.
> Kate: 20-30s [supporting role], clowns with husband, humorous bickering and joking, house in uproar because of continual redecorating.
> Jan: 20-30s, [supporting role], trendy, used to have a love relationship with Trevor.

BELL, BOOK AND CANDLE, John Van Druten (1951)   Dram. Pl. Ser.

2w 3m

Gillian a beautiful young witch casts a spell over a man to whom she is attracted. He falls madly in love, but she is unable to feel love for him until she renounces her witch powers. Comedy.

> Gillian: 27, [lead], graceful, beautiful, has supernatural powers.
> Miss Holroyd: 50s, [supporting role], comic, eccentric aunt, also a witch.

THE BELLE OF AMHERST, William Luce (1976)   Samuel French
1w

The sad life of Emily Dickinson from the age of 15 to her death
at 56 is beautifully told with many excerpts from her poetry.

> Emily: 53, [lead], looks younger than her years, eccentric
>   recluse, unhappy victim.

LES BELLES SOEURS, Michel Tremblay (1974)   Talonbooks
15w

A woman who has just won a million trading stamps holds a stamp
pasting party for her provincial, superstitious, Bingo fanatic
friends.   The party turns into a free-for-all when her envious
friends begin to steal her stamps.

> Germaine: late 30s-40s, [lead], winner of stamps, gloating,
>   sharp tongued, coarse, vulgar, abrasive.
> Rose: 44, [lead], sister of Germaine, narrow minded, bigot-
>   ed, judgmental, prudish, unhappily married.
> Gabrielle: early 40s, [supporting role], sister of Germaine,
>   nuts about contests, common, bossy.
> Pierette: 30, [supporting role], younger sister of Ger-
>   maine, kindly, caring, considered black sheep because she
>   works at a night club, feels washed-up and finished.
> Therese: 40s, [supporting role], stuck-up, smug because her
>   husband just got a raise, has to care for senile mother-
>   in-law.
> Olivine: 93, [short role], mother-in-law of Therese, comic,
>   continually falling out of wheelchair, infantile, bites
>   people.
> Angeline: 50s, [supporting role], lively, risque, goes to a
>   night club every Friday (considered immoral by her
>   friends), has arthritis.
> Rheauna: 50s, [supporting role], close friend of Angeline,
>   poor health, has had 17 operations, prudish, narrow mind-
>   ed.
> Lisette: 30s, [supporting role], puts on airs, been to
>   Europe, snobbish, embarrassed by the other women's be-
>   havior.
> Marie-Ange: late 30s-40s, [supporting role], overworked
>   housewife, jealous, bitter, resentful.
> Yvette: 40s, [supporting role], constantly talking about her
>   daughter's wedding and honeymoon.
> Des-Neiges: 30s, [supporting role], unmarried, desperately
>   lonely, in love with a door-to-door salesman she sees
>   once a month.
> Linda: teen-early 20s, [supporting role], Germaine's daugh-
>   ter, more progressive and modern than her mother, rebel-
>   lious, impatient.
> Lise: teen to early 20s, [supporting role], pregnant and
>   unmarried, ambitious, wanting to get out of her "fix" and
>   make a better life for herself.

Ginette: teen to early 20s, [short role], depressed, low
self esteem, feels inferior to her sister.

BERTHE, Michel Tremblay (1969)   Talonbooks
1w (1m offstage voice)

A movie theater ticket seller reveals her frustrations and fantasizes about becoming a popular film star. Short play.

Berthe: 50s-60s, [lead], garish, wears wildly shaped,
glittery blue plastic glasses, worldly, crude, disappointed with life.   ʼ

THE BICYCLE RIDERS, Anna Marie Barlow (1980) Best Short Plays 80
1w 1m

Two members of a bicycle riding act in their dressing room after
the show reveal their fears and hopes. Short play.

Patsy: 40s, [lead], whimsical, sprite, clown costumed.

BITS AND PIECES, Corrine Jacker (1975)   Dram. Pl. Ser.
3w 6m

A newly widowed woman whose husband donated his organs for medical transplants feels incomplete at his funeral and searches out
his scattered organs in their new bodies.

Iris: 30s, [lead], intelligent, distraught, committed to her
quest.
Helen: 30s, [supporting role], supportive sister-in-law.
Mrs. Eberly: 60s, [short role], homespun, brusque, zealously
religious, transplant recipient.

BLACK GIRL, J.E. Franklin (1969)   Dram. Pl. Ser.
6w 2m 1 girl 1 boy

The frustrations and struggles of Billie Jean as she tries to
make something of her life and become a ballet dancer in spite of
her family's resistance. Black cast.

Billie Jean: 18, [lead], hopeful, wanting more from life,
stressed by lack of support from family, talented dancer,
angry.
Norma: 21, [supporting role], older sister, intolerant of
Billie Jean's aspirations, slightly overweight, young
mother.
Ruth Ann: 20, [supporting role], older sister, mother of
young child.
Mama Rosie: 40-50s, [supporting role], tall, powerful, authoritarian.

Mu' Dear: 55, [short role], grandmother of Billie Jean, thin, short.

Netta: 20s, [short role], going to college to become a teacher.

Sheryl: 4, [short role], daughter of Ruth Ann.

BLANK PAGES, Frank Marcus (1973)   Best Short Plays 74
1w

Carole recounts her difficulties in her experiences with the opposite sex. Short play.

Carole: 25, [lead], attractive, plumpish, proper English, slightly self-deprecating, charming, witty.

BLIND DATE, Frank Marcus (1977)   Best Short Plays 79
1w 1m

Comic meeting at a railway station between a woman and a man who have been set up for a blind date but don't recognize each other. Short play.

Angie: early 20s, [lead], wears blue denim skirt, high black boots, lively, robust, impatient with herself for agreeing to the date.

BLOOD PHOTO, Edward Friedman (1969)   Chilton Book Co.
                                                   or Best Short Plays 69
3w 3m

The jealousy between two sisters sparks a highly charged emotional upheaval in an Italian family living in a New York City tenement. Short play.

Angela Benedetto: late 40s, [lead], looks older, huge, earthy mother, dominates family, simple yet shrewd and cunning.

Elizabeth Goodman: mid 20s, [supporting role], older daughter, attractive, refined, well balanced, intelligent, conservative dresser, college educated, married to writer.

Camille Benedetto: early 20s, [supporting role], younger daughter, a lot like her mother, plain, teased hair, common, wears fake fur.

BONJOUR LA BONJOUR, Michel Tremblay (1974)   Talonbooks
                                                   or John Goodwin
6w 2m

After a trip abroad a young man returns to his family (four doting older sisters, two older aunts, and a father), who can't

communicate, are unable to hear one another, and don't know what
to do about his incestuous relationship with his youngest sister.

> Albertine: 50-60s, [supporting role], aunt, watches TV con-
>   stantly.
> Charlotte: 50-60s, [supporting role], aunt, complains about
>   health, critical, suspicious, vindictive.
>
> the sisters:
> Lucienne: 40s, [supporting role], snobbish, status con-
>   scious, married to Englishman.
> Denise: 30s, [supporting role], overweight, compulsive over-
>   eater.
> Monique: 30s, [supporting role], hypochondriac, always tak-
>   ing pills, paranoid.
> Nicole: 30, [supporting role], youngest sister, kind, gen-
>   tle, loving, having sexual relationship with her brother.

BOSEMAN AND LENA, Athol Fugard (1969)   Samuel French
1w 2m

An itinerant black couple in South Africa struggle to make sense
of their lives. Black cast.

> Lena: 50s, [lead], tired, burdened, discouraged, depressed,
>   sad, has had a hard tedious life.

THE BRIDAL NIGHT, Paul Avila Mayer (1967)   Dram. Pl. Ser.
                                              or Best Short Plays 68
2w 4m

Lyrical tale set on the harsh Western coast of Ireland of a
young slow-witted man who has a deep passionate love for a
school teacher and goes mad when it doesn't work. Short play.

> Mrs. Sullivan: 60s, [lead], mother of mad man, narrates
>   action as well as takes part in it.
> Miss Regan: early 30s, [lead], good looking school teacher,
>   independent means, kindly, solitary, enjoys books.

BRINGING IT ALL BACK HOME, Terrance McNally (1969)
                                              Best Short Plays 69
3w 3m

Cutting satire of how a young man's death in Viet Nam affects his
family.   Mother is proud he was "American", father is proud he
was a "man". Short play. Black role.

> Mother: 40-50s, [supporting role], shallow, out of touch
>   with her feelings, main concern for son was that he was
>   patriotic.

Daughter: teens, [supporting role], mindless pom pom girl,
   chews gum, bickers with brother.
Miss Horne: 20s, [supporting role], svelte, black, TV news-
   caster, tough, outspoken, two personalities; one when on
   camera, another when off camera.

BRONTOSAURUS, Lanford Wilson (1978)   Dram. Pl. Ser.
2w 1m

A confrontation between an antique dealer and her callow nephew
is due to radically differing personalities; she is practical and
materialistic; he, mystical and reserved. Short play.

   Dealer: 40s, [lead], well dressed, cynical, wise-cracking,
      brittle.
   Assistant: 30-40s, [short role].

BUTTERFLIES ARE FREE, Leonard Gershe (1969)   Samuel French
2w 2m

A woman and man, neighbors in a grubby apartment building, become
good friends before she learns that he is blind.   His mother
tries to intervene, then reconsiders. Comedy.

   Jill: 19, [lead], lively, fresh, artsy, reading for a part
     in off-Broadway play, newly arrived from Los Angeles.
   Mrs. Baker: 40-50s, [supporting role], well dressed Scars-
     dale matron, upper middle class, worried about her son's
     ability to live alone.

CALIFORNIA SUITE, Neil Simon (1977)   Samuel French
2w 2m   (doubling of parts)

Four episodes each involving a different set of characters pass-
ing through a Beverly Hills hotel.

<u>Visitor from New York:</u> A sophisticated New Yorker tries unsuc-
cessfully to get custody of her daughter from former husband.

   Hannah: early 40s, [lead], well dressed, sharp, intelli-
     gent, anxious.

<u>Visitor from Philadelphia:</u> A wife catches her husband cheating.

   Millie: 40s, [supporting role], strong, forceful, practical,
     outraged, overcome with mighty wrath.

<u>Visitor from London:</u> An English film star nominated for an Acad-
emy Award has an argument with her husband.

   Diana: 40s, [lead], expensively dressed, anxious, intense,
     perfectionist.

<u>Visitors</u> <u>from</u> <u>Chicago:</u> Two couples who are fanatic tennis play-ers, comically squabble when one of the women gets an injury in a competitive tennis game.

>   Beth: 40s, [supporting role], comic, sophisticated, middle
>   class, has injured foot
>   Gert: 40s, [supporting role], comic, sophisticated, middle
>   class.

CALL ME JACKY   see   **A MATTER OF GRAVITY**

CALM DOWN MOTHER, Megan Terry (1965)   Samuel French
3w

Experimental biting piece in which three women go through sev-eral transformations; playing first a parody of one set of ster-eotyped female characters, then switching to different sets of characters.

CANADIAN GOTHIC, Joanna M. Glass (1977)   Dram. Pl. Ser.
2w 2m

A woman in a small, narrow-minded, Saskatchewan town in the 1950s falls in love with a Native American, becomes pregnant, and deals with the repercussions. Short play.

>   Jean: 30s, [lead], story flashes back to her youth, in con-
>   flict between creative, life-affirming, and practical,
>   limiting forces inside her.
>   Mother: 30s, [short role], loving, sensitive, independent,
>   capable, artistic.

CASTLE IN THE VILLAGE, Verna Woskoff (1958) Best Short Plays 58-9
3w 3m

A young woman renting out her apartment has several eager appli-cants with interesting backgrounds. Short play.

>   Lydia: 20s, [lead], warm hearted, glamorous.
>   Mrs. Goldfine: 50s, [supporting role], landlady, nervous,
>   out of breath.
>   Mrs. Hill: 20-30s, [short role], pregnant apartment seeker.

CATSPLAY, Istvan Orkeny (translated by Clara Gyorgyey) (1976)
                                             Samuel French
6w 3m

An eccentric older woman in Budapest describes her chaotic life as a widow and her subsequent romance.

Ersi: mid 60s, [lead], compassionate, agile, nervous.
Giza: late 60s, [lead], sister, in wheelchair, alert, calm, elegant.
Paula: early 60s, [supporting role], friend of Ersi, determined, commanding, crafty, manneristic.
Ilona: 30s, [short role], daughter, ambitious professional woman.
Mousie: late 50s, [short role], neighbor, shy, plain, loyal to Ersi.
Mrs. Adelaide Vivelli: 90s, [short role], ex-Wagnerian diva, haughty.

THE CHALK GARDEN, Enid Bagnold (1953)   Samuel French
7w 2m

A mysterious woman answers an ad for a companion to a 16 year-old girl living with her grandmother, is hired because of her uncanny knowledge of gardening, and becomes embroiled in household entanglements.

Madrigal: 30-40s, [lead], intense, neat, contained, calm, humorless, had been in prison, newly hired domestic, wins over granddaughter.
Mrs. St. Maugham: 60s, [lead], eccentric head of household, overpowering, indulgent towards her granddaughter.
Laurel: 16, [lead], insolent granddaughter, feels unloved, troubled about mother's new marriage.
Olivia: late 30s, [supporting role], well dressed, mother of Laurel, daughter of Mrs. St. Maugham, has remarried and lives abroad, wants to get her daughter back.
Second applicant: 30-40s, [short role], small, energetic, nervous, bird-like.
Third applicant: 50s, [short role], former beauty, great bearing, haughty.
Nurse: any age, [bit part].

CHAPTER TWO, Neil Simon (1977)   Samuel French
2w 2m

Romance between a woman recently divorced and a man recently widowed. Comedy.

Jennie Malone: 30s, [lead], wise, well-balanced, and chic.
Faye Medwick: 35, [supporting role], friend of Jennie, practical, witty, stage performer.

CHARACTER LINES, Larry Ketron (1979)   Dram. Pl. Ser.
2w 1m

Linda and Kit writers and former lovers find they still have strong feelings for each other seven years later, but they are on different paths. She has a best-selling novel, he has given up writing and works as a car mechanic.

> Linda: 37, [lead], successful novelist on publicity tour, feels guilty about abrupt departure from relationship seven years ago, pressured by demands of success.

> twin sisters played by same performer: 18, [supporting role]
> Evelyn: hangs around Kit's place with stories of flying saucers as an excuse to keep an eye on Kit.
> Ginger: having affair with Kit, bright, mature.

CHILDREN OF A LESSER GOD, Mark Medoff (1980)   Dram. Pl. Ser.
4w 3m

A teacher at a state school for the deaf marries one of his students and learns of the difficulties of being deaf from a closer perspective.

> Sarah: 26, [lead], deaf from birth, cannot speak and uses sign language to communicate, unwilling to learn to read lips, closes herself off from the hearing world, hostile, troubled, highly intelligent.
> Lydia: 20s, [supporting role], friend of Sarah, hearing impaired student, softer, reticent, frightened by Sarah.
> Mrs. Norman: 40-50s, [supporting role], Sarah's mother, discouraged, bitter, has given up on Sarah.
> Edna Klein: 20-30s, [supporting role], lawyer, naive and awkward around deaf people, hired as advocate for deaf rights.

THE CHINESE RESTAURANT SYNDROME, Corinne Jacker (1979)
                         Lois Berman or Best Short Plays 79
2w 1m

Two women, very close best friends, who have not seen each other for several years have a lunch time meeting in a restaurant.
Short play.

> Susan Lemmerer: 30s, [lead], chic, sophisticated, joking.
> Maggie Stewart: 30s, [lead], chic, sophisticated, glib, humorous.

CHOCOLATE CAKE, Mary Gallagher (1981)   Best Short Plays 82
2w

Two compulsive overeaters with very different personalities meet at a women's conference, and bond in a close friendship.
Short play.

> Delia: 40s, [lead], extrovert, ex-dancer, married to wealthy man, likable, crude, enjoys pinball, noise, and action.

Joellen: 27, [lead], slightly overweight, low-self image,
timid, small town, sells girdles at Penny's.

CLARA'S OLE MAN, Ed Bullins (1969)   Samuel French
                                        or Best Short Plays 69
4w 5m

The underside of life in South Philadelphia: Big Girl and Clara,
living together in a lesbian relationship, shelter three young
men running from the police. Short play. Black cast.
  Big Girl: 20-40s, [lead], heavy and powerful, bullies Clara,
    coarse, domineering, plain dresser.
  Clara: 18, [supporting role], slow, feline, good looking,
    submissive to Big Girl.
  Baby Girl: teen, [short role], mentally retarded sister of
    Big Girl, wears much make up, uses a lot of profanity.
  Miss Famie: 40-50s, [short role], alcoholic neighbor, thin.

A CLEARING IN THE WOODS, Arthur Laurents (1957)   Dram. Pl. Ser.
4w 5m 1 10-year-old girl

A woman tormented by the past relives memories in a clearing in
the wood, going through her emotional life with the loving support of a young scientist, until she finds peace in self acceptance.

  Virginia: 30, [lead], at a crisis in her life, intelligent,
    important job, over worked, hurting.
  Gina: (Virginia at 26), [lead], conscientious, edgy, hurt-
    ing, having marital problems, hard worker on job.
  Nora: (Virginia at 17), [supporting role], attractively
    dressed, idealistic, intellectual, rebellious.
  Jigee: (Virginia at 10), [supporting role], neatly dressed,
    white gloves, hat, glasses, needing love, angry at being
    neglected.
  Hazelmae: 17, [short role], friend of Nora, frivolous, pre-
    tentious, thick southern accent which is mostly affecta-
    tion, conventional, overweight.

CLOTHES FOR A SUMMER HOTEL, Tennessee Williams (1980)
                                        Dram. Pl. Ser.
9w 7m (can use doubling) + extras

F. Scott Fitzgerald and Zelda Sayre Fitzgerald relive memories
together and experience the pain their circumstances have brought
when he makes his last visit to her at the insane asylum.

  Zelda: 40s, [lead], once glamorous and very popular Southern
    belle, now put away in an insane asylum, fiery, unkempt,
    majestic.
  Sara Murphy: * [short role], old friend of Zelda.

Hadley Hemingway: * [short role], old friend of Zelda, wife
of Ernest.
Mrs. Patrick Campbell: past 50, [short role], famous stage
personality, sophisticated.
Sister One: any age, [short role], nun attendant at asylum.
Sister Two; any age, [short role], nun attendant at asylum.
Becky: age unspecified, [short role], patient at asylum.
Boo-Boo: age unspecified, [short role], demented patient in
wheelchair.
Nurse; age unspecified, [short role].

*Sara and Hadely appear as memories from the past and their ages
could range anywhere from 20s to 40s.

THE COAL DIAMOND, Shirley Lauro (1978)   Dram. Pl. Ser.
                                         or Best Short Plays 80
4w

A conversation during a lunch time bridge game at an insurance
company office reveals personal secrets. Short play.

Inez: mid 20s to mid 30s, [lead], tall, thin, awkward, chews
gum and smokes Camels.
Lena: late 40s to 50s, [lead], the boss, wears a girdle,
hose, pumps, and a rayon print dress.
Betty Jean: 19, [lead], peroxide blonde, pregnant, wears
pink and white maternity smock.
Pearl: mid 20s to mid 30s, [lead], new in town, feels she is
less intelligent than the others.

THE COCKTAIL PARTY, T.S. Elliot (1950)   Samuel French
4w 4m

A party given by a married couple who are about to separate has a
mysterious guest who stimulates revelations for the others.
British.

Julia: 50-60s, [supporting role], worldly socialite, poised,
sophisticated.
Celia: 20-30s, [supporting role], confused, searching, in
love with Lavinia's husband.
Lavinia: 20-30s, [supporting role], has just left her husband.
Nurse secretary: [short role].

COME INTO THE GARDEN, MAUD, Noel Coward (1966)   Samuel French
2w 2m

The husband of a shallow pretentious social-climber finds solace
with a gentle, unpretentious, penniless princess. Short play.

Anna-Mary: late 40s-50s, [supporting role], snobbish, dressed expensively, petty.

Maud: late 40s, [supporting role], intelligent, attractive,
     sophisticated, from European royalty, individualistic,
     inner confidence.

COMPANIONS OF THE FIRE, Ali Wadud (1980)   Dram. Pl. Ser.
1w 1m

An older woman invites a young man up to her Harlem apartment.
Short play. Black cast.

     Woman: 50s, [lead], fun-loving, wears an obvious wig, very
          fat, lets herself be victimized.

CONFESSIONS OF A FEMALE DISORDER, Susan Miller (1973)
                                             Gay Plays or Flora Roberts
8w 7m (doubling) + extras

A woman's journey to maturity and self acceptance from adolescence, through her college years, to young adulthood. Her quest
leads to a lesbian relationship with her former college roommate. Sexually explicit language.

     Ronnie: late 20s, [lead], searching for identity, time span
          from puberty to late 20s.
     Coop: late 20s [lead], roommate of Ronnie, in love with her,
          free spirit.
     Evelyn: 30-40s [short role], very depressed housewife, next
          door neighbor, (good monologue material).
     Liz: 20s [short role], college roommate of Ronnie and Coop.
     Cheerleaders 1, 2, & 3: 20s, [supporting role], these women
          play together as an ensemble in several short scenes.
     Woman 1, 2, 3, & 4: 3 in 20s, 1 in 40s, [short role], each
          has a short speech describing her life situation. Actors
          playing cheerleaders are doubled here.

THE CORRUPTERS, Gertrude Samuel (1969)   Best Short Plays 69
8w 8m

An ex-con and prostitute/drug addict fails to make it in the out-
side world, is sent back to prison, and meets her end there.
Short play.

     Carol Ramirez: late teens, [lead], convict with long record
          of drug crimes and prostitution.
     Rachel Crane: 30s, [supporting role], reporter, middle
          class, intelligent, advocate for Carol.
     Boots: teens-30s, [supporting role], tough boss of prison
          inmates, mean, domineering.
     Mary: teens-30s, [supporting role], prison inmate, befriends
          Carol, fearful.
     Frankie: teens-30s, [supporting role], prison inmate, rough
          cohort of Boots.

Liz: teens-30s, [short role], prison inmate, scared of Boots.
Marie Caliante: 17, [short role], young prostitute up before the judge.
Prison Guard: 30-40s, [short role].

A COUPLA WHITE CHICKS SITTING AROUND TALKING, John F. Noonan (1981)   Samuel French
2w

After some difficulties, a Westchester housewife befriends her new neighbor, and together they comically conspire to get even with their philandering husbands. Comedy.

Maude Mix: 20-50, [lead], typical New York suburban house-wife.
Hannah Mae Bindler: 20-50, [lead], newly arrived wife from Texas.

CRAB DANCE, Beverly Simons (1969)   Beverly Simons
1w 3m

A character study of unique Sadie Golden on an afternoon which brings three visitors.

Sadie Golden: 50s, [lead], "tall, thin, sagging, with gray streaked black hair", coarse, blunt.

CRIMES OF THE HEART, Beth Henley (1981)   Viking Penguin
4w 2m

Set in a small Mississippi town this is a story of a young woman who has just shot her husband and the resulting crisis in her family. Pulitzer Prize winner.

Lenny McGrath: 30, [lead], plump, painfully shy with men, self-conscious, easily embarrassed, responsible, self sacrificing, lonely.
Meg McGrath: 27, [lead], unstable, wild, former nightclub singer, bad reputation in town, favored child in family, traumatic childhood.
Babe McGrath: 24, [lead], shot husband who brutalized her, scared, frightened, unsophisticated, loving, likable.
Chick: 29, [supporting role], neighbor, cousin, garish, overly concerned for propriety and status, judgmental, critical, prudish.

CROWN MATRIMONIAL, Royce Ryton (1973)   The Dramatic Pub. Co.
                                                  or Plays of the Year vol. 43
6w 3m

The story of Queen Mary's experiences leading up to the abdica-
tion of her son, Edward VIII, from the throne of England in 1937.

>   Queen Mary: 69, [lead], stately monarch, great dignity,
>   proper, traditional, recently widowed, deeply upset by
>   son's actions.
>   Lady Arlie (Mabell): 60s, [supporting role], lady in wait-
>   ing, confidant and loyal friend to the queen.
>   Mary, Princess Royal: 39, [supporting role], dutiful, loyal
>   to her mother and the monarchy, reserved.
>   Duchess of York (Elizabeth): 36, [supporting role], pretty,
>   dignified, well-mannered, charming, slightly plump, mar-
>   ried to king's brother.
>   Duchess of Glouster (Alice): 34, [short role], attractive,
>   very shy, sensible.
>   Margaret Wyndham: 60s, [short role], lady in waiting,
>   traditional, set in her ways.

THE CURIOUS SAVAGE, John Patrick (1950)   Dram. Pl. Ser.
6w 5m

Mrs. Savage is committed to a sanatarium by her conniving children trying to get control of her money, makes meaningful friend-
ships there, and wins out in the end. Comedy.

>   Mrs. Savage: 60s, [lead], sensible, loving, committed to the
>   human spirit, energetic zest for life, individualistic.
>   Lily Belle: early 40s, [supporting role], vain, self-assur-
>   ed, smart, harsh, step-daughter eager to put mother away.
>   Wilhelmina: mid 20s, [supporting role], attractive, effi-
>   cient, professional, staff of sanatarium.
>
>   Patients at sanatarium:
>   Fairy May: early 20s, [supporting role], beauty hid by
>   severe hair style and dress.
>   Florence: late 20s, [supporting role], sweet, graceful,
>   eager to please.
>   Mrs. Paddy: 50s, [supporting role], eccentric artist/paint-
>   er, stout, pudgy, ferocious, aggressive.

THE DANCERS, Horton Foote (1955)   Dram. Pl. Ser.
7w 3m

A nostalgic piece set in a small Texas town dealing with the
problems of two young people struggling to find confidence in
themselves. Short play.

>   Mary Catherine: 17-18, [supporting role], believes she is
>   plain and not as popular as her friends, kindly, loyal,

generous, her family cannot afford to send her to college.

Emily: 17-18, [supporting role], Mary Catherine's friend,
the most popular girl in town, has beautiful clothes.

Inez: 30s, [supporting role], tries to arrange dates for her
younger brother, overprotective and worried about him,
pressures him to have fun.

Mrs. Davis: 40s, [supporting role], mother of Mary Catherine, pleased with her daughter.

Elizabeth: 40s, [supporting role], mother of Emily, pressures Emily to date brother of Inez, worried about what
Inez will think.

Waitress: age unspecified, [short role], works in drugstore.

Velma: 17, [short role], friend of Mary Catherine.

THE DARK OF THE MOON AND THE FULL, Joseph Hart (1974)

Best Short Plays 77

4w 1m

In the Irish-Catholic section of Brooklyn on a Good Friday, an
old woman goes mad reliving incidents from her life in Dublin in
1916 which included a passionate love affair. Short play.

Grandma: 70s, [lead], family monarch, sardonic, crafty, mischievous, full of the devil, drinks too much.

Helen: 40s, [supporting role], daughter of Grandma, stout,
strong, cheerful, peasant-like.

Patsy: 17, [supporting role], granddaughter, slim, graceful, pretty, lively, hip-chic dress.

Loretta: 40s, [short role], efficient, serious, strained.

THE DARNING NEEDLE, Donald Kvares (1978)

Best Short Plays 78
or Harold Freeman

2w 1m

An evening's gin game turns into a seance as the spirit of Ida's
mother tries to communicate, coming back in the form of an in-
sect. Short play.

Betty: 40-50s, [lead], tough, practical, abrasive, uneducated, simple, coarse.

Ida: 40-50s, [lead], a dressmaker for many years, affable,
interested in astrology and the occult, psychic.

A DAY IN THE LIFE OF JOE EGG see JOE EGG

A DELICATE BALANCE, Edward Albee (1966)

Samuel French

4w 2m

A middle-aged couple's stability is shaken by a visit from their
best friends (mysteriously in a state of shock needing to stay

with them), and the return of their 36-year-old daughter just breaking up from her fourth marriage. Pulitzer Prize winner.

> Agnes: late 50s, [lead], good-looking, dresses elegantly, nervous, tightly controlled emotions, cool, superior attitude.
> Claire: late 40-50s, [supporting role], alcoholic sister of Agnes, out-spoken, warm, earthy, vulgar, spontaneous.
> Edna: late 50s, [supporting role], long time friend of Agnes, overcome with fear, staying at Agnes' house.
> Julia: mid 30s, [supporting role], spoiled daughter of Agnes, irritable, agitated, her fourth marriage has just fallen apart.

DENTIST AND PATIENT, William Saroyan (1968)   Best Short Plays 68
2w (originally written for 2m)

An encounter between a dentist and her patient illustrates the premise that wealthy people cheat and take advantage of others to get ahead. Short play.

> Anybody: age unspecified, [lead], naive dentist, honest, gullible chump.
> Anybody else: age unspecified, [lead], the patient, millionaire, crafty, unscrupulous, stingy.

DESIGN FOR LIVING, Noel Coward (1933)   Samuel French
4w 5m

The high spirited story of the merry adventures of Gilda as she bounces back and forth between two lovers. Comedy.

> Gilda: 30, [lead], fun loving, gay, smart, sophisticated.
> Helen Carver: 20s, [short role], conservative, wealthy, well-dressed.
> Grace Torrence: 30-40s, [short role], sophisticated, "Europeanized New York matron".
> Miss Hodge: any age, [short role], untidy, comic servant.

THE DRAPES COME, Charles Dezenzo (1964)   Dram. Pl. Ser.
2w

Absurdist treatment of relationship between an aggressive teen aged girl and her meek timid mother who switch personalities back and forth.

> Mrs. Fiers: 40-50s, [lead], mother, likable, kind, meek, then changes to domineering, nasty, abrasive,
> Barbara: 17, [lead], daughter, high school senior, first harsh, cruel, disorderly, heartless, then changes to timid, withdrawn, and fearful.

LA DUCHESSE DE LANGEAIS, Michel Tremblay (1970)   Talonbooks
1w

A retired prostitute talks about her colorful adventures around the world as she drinks herself into oblivion. Sexually explicit language.

> La Duchesse: 60s, [lead], coarse, outspoken, vulgar, tough, sophisticated, continental, lively.

DUSA, FISH, STAS, AND VI, Pam Gems (1977)   Dram. Pl. Ser.
4w

Three women sharing a flat in London and a friend struggle to overcome tragic circumstances in their lives.

> Violet: teens, [lead], waif, punkish, physically weak, recuperating from illness, sometimes on uppers.
> Dusa: 20s, [lead], artistic, intelligent, husband has run off with their two children.
> Fish: 20s, [lead], from upper middle class background, intelligent, active in political causes, lover has left her for another.
> Stas: 20s, [lead], big, attractive, physiotherapist, very intelligent, loves science, raising money for college education by being call girl at night.

EDUCATING RITA, Willy Russell (1980)   Samuel French
1w 1m

A common hairdresser wishing to get an education enrolls in a free University course, is tutored by a middle-aged, jaded professor, and undergoes a drastic transformation.

> Rita: 26, [lead], passionate about learning, changes from garish to ultra sophisticate, from insecure to confident, from fresh and innocent to blasé.

THE EFFECT OF GAMMA RAYS ON MAN-IN-THE-MOON MARIGOLDS,
     Paul Zindel (1970)   Dram. Pl. Ser.
5w

The shy daughter of an embittered poverty-stricken widow gains recognition for her scientific experiment with growing marigolds.

> Beatrice: late 40s, [lead], angry, resentful, unkempt widow struggling to support self and two daughters.
> Ruth: teens, [lead], older daughter, high-strung, pretty, shallow, not very bright, a little strange.
> Tillie: teens, [lead], younger daughter, shy, plain, highly intelligent, has talent for science.

Janice: teens, [short role], pompous winner of science prize.
Nanny: very old, [short role], senile, non speaking.

EVERYBODY HAS TO BE SOMEBODY, Helen McAvity (1971) Dram. Pl. Ser.
3w 1m   3 14-year-old boys

A stage mother learns to give up her aspirations for her daughter and comes to the decision to allow her daughter to live her own life.

Maggie: 60s, [lead], vivid, honest, direct, domineering and somewhat overbearing, energetic, sense of humor, runs her daughter's household.
Frances: 30s, [supporting role], Maggie's daughter, pretty, had been a child star, dresses simply, shy, modest, values her privacy and her family life.
Birdie: 60s, [supporting role], old friend of Maggie, also stage mother, well dressed, wealthy, gentle, sincere, lonely.

EVERYBODY LOVES OPAL   see **OPAL SERIES**

THE EYE OF THE BEHOLDER, Kent Broadhurst (1982)   Dram. Pl. Ser.
3w (originally written for 3m)

Two artists sharing a studio bicker about art techniques and their differing philosophies of life as they paint at their easels. Short play.

Jane: over 30, [lead], slim, fair, intellectual, artistic style cool and classical.
Bella: over 30, [lead], heavy set, dark, emotional, artistic style intense, free, loose, abandoned.
Leona: over 30, [supporting role], model, attractive, opinionated, joins in conversation.

FALLEN ANGELS, Noel Coward (1925)   Samuel French
3w 3m

The gay intrigues of two women beginning to get bored with their marriages when an old lover they had in common comes to town.

Jane: 30s, [lead], sophisticated, upper class, attractive, chic, light hearted.
Julia: 30s, [lead], sophisticated, upper class, attractive, chic, light hearted.

FATHER'S DAY, Oliver Hailey (1970)   Dram. Pl. Ser.
3w   3m

Three   divorced women invite their former husbands to a   cocktail
party. Comedy.

>   Louise: 30s, [lead], lean, good-looking, cynical and bitter.
>   Estelle: early 30s, [lead], fragile, soft.
>   Marian: 30s, [lead], tall, dark, articulate, severe.

FAVOURITE NIGHTS, Stephen Poliakoff, (1982)   Methuen
3w 4m

A   London   West End gambling casino is setting for examining   the
conflicts   of   an over-qualified language instructor who   teaches
wealthy foreign businessmen to speak English.

>   Catherine: late 20s: [lead], striking looking, honest, di-
>   rect, English instructor, knowledgeable, intellectually
>   gifted, excelled in school, cool, self-contained.
>   Sarah: early 20s, [supporting role], Catherine's younger
>   sister, anxiously awaiting the results of her exams, not
>   as bright as her sister, naive, worried.
>   The girl: 20s, [short role], casino employee.

FEFU AND HER FRIENDS, Maria Irene Fornes, 1977   Bertha Case
8w

Fefu entertains a group of friends who have come together to plan
a presentation. (The performing space is divided up to represent
the rooms and garden of a house, and the audience is divided up
into four groups during the second act and circulates to view
scenes playing simultaneously in four different rooms.)

>   Fefu: [lead], 20s, crazy in an absurd way, plays with guns,
>   has strange marriage.
>   Cindy: [supporting role], 20s, close friend of Fefu, loyal,
>   tolerant, good singing voice.
>   Christine: [supporting role], 20s, timid, conformist, child-
>   ish, reads French.
>   Julia: [supporting role], 20s, traumatized by a hunting
>   accident, paralyzed in wheelchair, having hallucinations,
>   ultimate victim.
>   Emma: [supporting role], 20s, concerned about sex, outgoing.
>   Paula: [supporting role], 20s, discouraged about her love
>   relationship, sings Schubert's Who is Sylvia?
>   Cecilia: [supporting role], 20s, intelligent, self assured.
>   Sue: [supporting role], 20s, humorous, clowns.

FINISHING TOUCHES, Jean Kerr (1973)   Dram. Pl. Ser.
3w 5m

Sentimental comedy about a married couple tempted with extra-
marital relationships.

    Katy: 40, [lead], wife and mother, literate, quick-witted,
        with a sarcastic edge, a bit dowdy.
    Felicia: 26, [supporting role], beautiful, charming, flir-
        tatious, theatrical affectations, from wealthy family.
    Elsie: 22, [supporting role], student, big hearted, attrac-
        tive, not very bright.

FIRST BREEZE OF SUMMER, Leslie Lee (1975)   Samuel French
6w 8m

The heart warming tale of a matriarch of a black family recalling
her past as her family moves into the middle class. Black cast.

    Gremmar: 70s, [supporting role], religious, conservative,
        has frequent reveries in the past.
    Aunt Edna: 50s, [supporting role], daughter of Gremmar,
        earthy, lively.
    Hattie: 50s, [supporting role], daughter-in-law, tease.
    Lucretia: late teens, [supporting role], Gremmar in her
        youth, beautiful, servant.
    Gloria: late 30s, [short role], angry, believes she has been
        cheated.
    Hope: early 20s, [short role], girl friend of grandson.

FIRST MONDAY IN OCTOBER, Jerome Lawrence,   Robert E. Lee (1978)
                                          Samuel French
2w 13m

The first woman on the Supreme Court a right-winger falls into a
lively rivalry and sparring match with a liberal colleague.
Comedy.

    Ruth Loomis: 40-50s, [lead], attractive, lawyer and newly
        appointed justice of the Supreme Court, quick-witted,
        high moral principles, politically conservative.
    Miss Birnbaum: any age, [short role], secretary of Supreme
        Court Justice, has frequent colds.

THE FLOUNDER COMPLEX, Anthony Damato (1968)   Dram. Pl. Ser.
2w

A young girl answers an ad for a servant for an old woman who is
nearly blind and extremely paranoid. The woman, after revealing
herself, believes that she cannot let the girl leave. Thriller.

Woman: 54, [lead], sneaky, conniving, almost blind, sententious, bigoted, paranoid, violent.
Girl: 19, [supporting role], sweet, easy going, kind, pretty, modest, average.

FOR COLORED GIRLS WHO HAVE CONSIDERED SUICIDE WHEN THE RAINBOW IS ENUF, Ntozake Shange (1975)   Samuel French
7w

Poetry and dance are combined in a self-exploration of a woman revealing seven facets of her personality as she celebrates being black and female.

FOR THE USE OF THE HALL, Oliver Hailey (1976)   Dram. Pl. Ser.
4w 2m

Martin, the author of a play that just flopped on Broadway, retreats to the family summer house on Long Island where he encounters a former lover, and old friend, and his sister who are all experiencing crises in their lives.

Bess: 60-80s, [supporting role], mother of Terry and Martin, elegant, authoritative, narrates action.
Charlotte: early 40s, [lead], former lover of Martin, tall, graceful, Bryn Mawr graduate, chic, penniless because her husband's fortune is exhausted, critical, bitter and harsh, resorting to stealing food, wears a fur coat to keep out the cold.
Terry: late 30s, [supporting role], Martin's sister, long red hair, plump, nun from a progressive order, wears a pant suit, questioning her vocation and relationship to God, tender hearted.
Alice: late 30s, [supporting role], blond, bosomy, cheerful, living with Martin, supportive of him, writes children books, practical, survivor.

FORTY CARATS, Jay Allen (1968)   Samuel French
6w 5m

A youthful forty year old woman has a romance with a twenty-two year old man mature for his age. Comedy.

Ann Stanley: 40, [lead], attractive, practical, successful real estate broker.
Maud Hayes: 60s, [supporting role], Ann's mother, lively, nutty, conniving, borrows clothes from granddaughter.
Trina Stanley: 17, [supporting role], Ann's daughter, hip, pool-hustler, easy going, casual.
Mrs. Latham: late 40s-50s, [supporting role], mother of Ann's lover, youthful for age, elegant, wealthy.
Mrs. Margolin: any age, [short role], secretary.
Mrs. Adams: any age, [very short role], customer.

FRIDAY NIGHT   see **THE RIVER**

THE FROGS, Eunice Hanger (1950-60s)   <u>2D</u> <u>and</u> <u>other</u> <u>Plays</u>
3w

Set in the Australian outback, this tale shows a gentle but
determined city woman struggling with unusual hardships learning
to succeed as a wheat farmer's wife. Short play.

> Maisie: 22, [lead], slim, pretty, bright, efficient, tender
>   hearted, gentle, city bred.
> Mrs. Tupper: 50s, [lead], overweight mother-in-law of
>   Maisie, critical but affable, raised in the bush.
> Miss Phillips: 30s, [lead], sturdy, raised in the bush,
>   teacher in local school, sensitive, aware.

FUNNYHOUSE OF A NEGRO, Adrienne Kennedy (1970)   Samuel French
5w 3m

Expressionistic treatment of the hallucinations of a woman going
mad and getting ready to hang herself. Black roles. Short play.

> Sarah: age unspecified, [lead], [black], insane, hallucina-
>   ting, angry, long monologues.
> Queen Victoria: 40-60s, [supporting role], has back to au-
>   dience, wears white mask, never moves.
> Duchess of Hapsburg: 40-60s, [supporting role], has back to
>   audience, wears white mask, never moves.
> Landlady: 30-50s, [supporting role], tall, thin, white wom-
>   an, long monologue.

GERTRUDE STEIN, GERTRUDE STEIN, GERTRUDE STEIN, Marty Martin
    (1979)   Random House
1w

Award winning depiction of Gertrude Stein in 1938, describing her
life at the center of a circle of artists, writers, and American
ex-patriots in Paris in the twenties.

> Gertrude Stein: 64, [lead], brilliant writer, large, over-
>   weight, powerful, unconventional, individualist, avant
>   garde collector of art.

GETTING OUT, Marsha Norman (1978)   Dram. Pl. Ser.
5w 7m

The struggle of an ex-con to avoid bad influences from former
associates and make a new life for herself.

> Arlene: late 20s, [lead], subdued, just finished an eight

year jail term for murder, had been a prostitute, vic-
timized by old associates.
Arlie: teen or early 20s, [supporting role], younger version
of Arlene, spirited and violent.
Ruby: late 30s, [supporting role], friend and ex-con, tries
to help.
Arlie's mother: 50s, [supporting role], taxi-driver, bitter,
withholds love from her daughter.
School principal: any age, [short role].

GIFT OF MURDER!, George Batson (1974)   Dram. Pl. Ser.
5w 3m

A high-living famous stage personality comes to a cottage in
northern England for rest and recuperation. Romance, mystery,
and murder follow. Comedy-thriller.

Stella: 50s, [lead], famous star, jagged nerves, on the
wagon, throws temper tantrums, sympathetic, likable.
Flavia: 40-50s, [supporting role], Stella's theatrical
rival, tall, vain, arresting, acid, biting wit.
Nurse: ageless, [supporting role], unlimited curiosity,
energetic, secretly resentful, impersonator.
Mary: early 20s, [supporting role], pretty, wholesome, niece
of Stella.
Wimpie: 50s, [supporting role], efficient housekeeper, outspoken.

THE GIN GAME, D.L. Coburn (1977)   Samuel French
1w 1m

As two nursing home residents get to know one another during a
series of card games, their anger mounts and they tear at each
other's facades. Comedy.

Fonsia: 71, [lead], new resident to home, timid, lonely,
has diabetes, self-righteous, judgmental, rigid, lucky at
cards.

THE GINGERBREAD LADY, Neil Simon (1971)   Samuel French
3w 3m

A singer just back from a sanatarium for alcoholics fights to
survive amid well-meaning friends who only make things worse.

Evy: 40s, [lead], alcoholic singer, glamorous, nervous,
outgoing, sexy.
Toby: early 40s, [supporting role], looks much younger,
friend of Evy, pretty, well-dressed.
Polly: 17, [supporting role], Evy's daughter, down-to-earth,
pretty, long, straight hair.

GOD SAYS THERE IS NO PETER OTT, Bill Hare (1972)   Dram. Pl. Ser.
3w 2m

A woman who runs a guest house on Cape Cod is joined by her
niece: an un-wed, expectant mother, soon to deliver. Complica-
tions arise at the appearance of the child's father.
Comedy- drama.

> Avis: 40s, [lead], plain, carelessly dressed, drinker, "eyes
>   and manner of a tough but whimsical poker player"
> Mary: 21, [lead], pretty, sullen and spoiled, expensively
>   dressed.
> Marcia: 40s, [short role], Mary's narrow minded mother,
>   smartly dressed.

GOING TO SEE THE ELEPHANT, Karen Hensel, Patti Johns, Elana Kent,
    Sylvia Meredith, Elizabeth Lloyd Shaw, Laura Toffenetti
    (1982)   West Coast Plays #15/16
4w 1m

This tale describes the life and hardships of the sod house
dwellers in the plains of Kansas in the 1870s.

> Maw Wheeler: 60-70s, [lead], energetic, strong willed, worn
>   face, "sure of her own moral and intellectual superior-
>   ity".
> Sara Wheeler: 26-28, [lead], Maw's daughter-in law, whole-
>   some, earthy, sincere, kind, mother of two small child-
>   ren, long hair, good singing voice (sings several songs).
> Etta Bailey; 22, [lead], grew up on prairies, child like,
>   unaffected, strange, stoic, has experienced severe trau-
>   ma.
> Helene Nichols: 35, [lead], raised in New York, refined,
>   Victorian, graceful, under strain because of hardships.

GOLDA, William Gibson (1977)   Samuel French
5w 18m (doubling)

An aging Golda Meir now Prime Minister of Israel dealing with the
Yom Kipper war, looks back over her life and the events that
brought her to her present situation. The lead performer plays
Golda in later life, (50s through 70s) and another plays Golda in
her younger years. The other appearances are short and much
doubling is employed.

> Golda: 50s, (action spans over her entire life) [lead],
>   determined, idealistic, formidable administrator, com-
>   passionate.
> Lou: middle aged, [short role], also plays Clara middle
>   aged, and DP.
> Small girl: [short role], Golda as a young child, also plays
>   Sarile as a child, and DP.

Sister: teen, [short role], also plays young girl, Clara
    teen aged, American girl, DP.
Mother: middle aged, [short role], also plays third witness,
    Sarile middle aged, DP.

A GOOD TIME, Ernest Thompson (1977)   Dram. Pl. Ser.
                                                 or Best Short Plays 80
1w 1m

A woman in New York City is surprised by a visit from a
California highway patrolman whom she promised two and a half
years earlier to show "a good time" when he came to New York.
Comedy. Short play.

Mandy Morgan: early 30s, [lead], chic, a ballet dancer of
    moderate skill, cynical, disillusioned, sharp, witty,
    lonely.

GOODBYE MY FANCY, Fay Kanin (1947)   Samuel French
12w 8m

A congresswoman returns to her Alma Mater to receive an honorary
degree, bringing a controversial war film to exhibit, and becomes
disillusioned with the idol of her college years. Comedy.

Agatha Reed: 40s, [lead], intelligent, successful, tough,
    idealistic, congresswoman with a sentimental streak.
Ellen Griswold: 40s, [supporting role], old roommate of
    Agatha, former beauty, now overweight, not scholarly,
    superficial.
Grace Woods: 50s, [supporting role], top notch secretary,
    very knowledgeable about the Washington scene.
Ginny Merrill: early 20s, [supporting role], serious minded
    student, daughter of college president.
Mary Nell: early 20s, [supporting role], Ginny's roommate,
    not interested in studies, superficial.
Miss Shakleford: 60-70s, [supporting role], alumnae secre-
    tary, harsh, over concerned about propriety.

THE GREAT NEBULA IN ORION, Lanford Wilson (1971)   Dram. Pl. Ser.
                                                 or Best Short Plays 72
2w

Two girlhood friends meet by chance and discuss their present
lives. One has a successful career, the other a "good marriage",
but both feel something is missing. Short play.

Carrie: early 30s, [lead], well dressed, plumpish, suburban
    wife and mother.
Louise: early 30s, [lead], successful dress designer, well
    dressed, smart, hints at lesbianism.

HAY FEVER, Noel Coward (1925)   Samuel French
5w 4m

A well known performer, her author husband, and their two adult
children intimidate and alienate house guests with their wittily
unconventional, free-wheeling ways. British comedy.

> Judith Bliss: late 40-50s, [lead], retired performer, glam-
>   orous in eccentric way, enjoys making extravagant drama-
>   tizations about her domestic situations, delights in
>   making scenes for amusement.
> Sorel Bliss: 19, [lead], her mother's daughter, but more
>   conventional and concerned for propriety, attractive.
> Myra Arundel: 30s [supporting role], ultra chic, fashion-
>   able, sophisticated guest.
> Jackie Coryton: 20s, [supporting role], plain, ingenuous,
>   simple guest.

THE HORSE LATITUDES, Stephen Black (1975)   Dram. Pl. Ser.
                                         or Best Short Plays 76
2w 1m 1 boy

A woman caught up in memories and illusions idles away an afternoon at an old railway station with her two children. Short play.

> Neva Jo: 35, [lead], lives in fantasy.
> Mary: 15, [supporting role], daughter, bookworm, sensitive.

HOT L BALTIMORE, Lanford Wilson (1973)   Dram. Pl. Ser.
7w 8m

Derelict residents of a soon to be demolished hotel share their
stories and prepare to leave the hotel.

> Milly: late 60s, [supporting role], used to wait tables, has
>   ability to see ghosts, spaced out.
> Mrs. Billotti: aging, [supporting role], mother of a thief
>   who was evicted from the hotel.
> April: 30 plus, [supporting role], beautiful, brassy prosti-
>   tute.
> Jackie: 25, [supporting role], violent, fighter, thief,
>   dreamer.
> Suzy: 30 plus, [supporting role], prostitute, "Jewish Mari-
>   lyn Monroe".
> Girl: 17, [supporting role], sensitive, pretty, prostitute.
> Mrs. Oxenham: 45, [short role], no nonsense desk clerk.

HOW THE OTHER HALF LOVES, Alan Ayckbourn (1971)   Samuel French
3w 3m

Funny romantic entanglements result when discovery threatens an
affair between a man and the wife of a co-worker. Comedy.

> Theresa Phillips: 30s, [supporting role], feels inadequate,
>   frustrated with her life.
> Fiona Foster: 30-40s, [supporting role], well-off, smart and
>   sophisticated, having affair with younger man, (Theresa's
>   husband).
> Mary Detweiler: 30s, [supporting role], nervous, insecure,
>   timid, bites nails.

I AM A CAMERA, John Van Druten (1952)   Dram. Pl. Ser.
4w 3m

Portrait of extravagantly confident irresponsible Sally Bowes in
Berlin 1930.

> Sally: 18-25, [lead], childlike tart, sexually amoral,
>   self centered, full of life, from upper class British
>   family.
> Fraulein: 40s, [supporting role], broad build, lusty humor,
>   feels sorry for herself, intimately friendly, supports
>   Nazis.
> Mrs. Watson-Courtneidge: 40-50s, [short role], Sally's
>   mother, genteel, British matron, attempting to be broad
>   minded, indulges Sally, comic.
> Natalia: 22, [short role], intensely serious, searching for
>   the truth, decisive, German formality.

I JUST WANTED SOMEONE TO KNOW, Bette Craig, Joyce Kornbluh (1981)
                                             Smyrna Press
20+w 1-2m (can use doubling)

Based on oral history sources a series of short monologues and
scenes documents the struggles, pain, and heroism of working
women in America and their contribution to the labor movement.
Black, Hispanic, and Hawaiian roles. Short play.

> all roles: short appearances.

I LOST A PAIR OF GLOVES YESTERDAY, Myrna Lamb (1972)
                    Howard Rosenstone or New Woman's Theater
1w

A flustered performer shuffles through her script, intimately
shares past experiences, and mentions that her father died a
couple of weeks ago.

An Actress: over 30, [lead], tired, despairing, discouraged, but has flashes of vivaciousness and energy.

I OUGHT TO BE IN PICTURES, Neil Simon (1980)   Samuel French
2w 1m

A 19-year-old woman, ostensibly aspiring to become a Hollywood star, travels to California to visit her father who left home when she was too young to remember and settles her personal account with him.

> Libby: 19, [lead], angry daughter of divorced parents, competent, caring, independent, very mature for her age, perceptive.
> Steffy: 40s, [supporting role], attractive, single mother dating Libby's father, putting up with poor treatment, neglect and indifference from him.

IMPROMPTU, Tad Mosel (1961)   Dram. Pl. Ser.
2w 2m

A group of actors on an empty stage waiting for the stage manager to arrive reveal their personal conflicts and share some intimate secrets.

> Winifred: 30s, [lead], brittle, cynical, glamorous, seasoned performer.
> Lora: late teens-early 20s, [supporting role], innocent naive, accommodating.

IN THE DESSERT OF MY SOUL, John Glines (1971)   Dram. Pl. Ser.
                                                  or Best short Plays 76
2w 2m

The owner of a dessert shack: a coarse, earthy, old woman, has a visit from a stranger and arranges a match between him and a young woman staying with her.

> Ma: 50-70s, [lead], tough, foul-mouthed, blunt, but caring.
> Josie: 20s, [supporting role], had tough life without love from family and found it with men.

INDEPENDENCE DAY, see **TODAY IS INDEPENDENCE DAY**

THE INDEPENDENT FEMALE, Joan Holden, (1970)   San Francisco
    Mime Troupe   or A Century of Plays by American Women
3-4w 2-3m

A comic melodrama depicting the dire consequences that befall society when women assert their independence. Short play.

Sarah Bullit: 25, [lead], outspoken feminist, dedicated,
    quick witted, angry.
Gloria Pennybank: 22, [lead], impressionable, childish,
    naive, preparing to be married, confused.
Matilda Pennybank: 53, [supporting role], mother of Gloria,
    petty, trite, firmly believes that women should be
    subservient to men.
Barker: any age, [short role], makes introductory speech at
    beginning of action and sums up at the end of play.

JACOB'S LADDER, Barbara Graham (1979)   West Coast Plays #6
2w 2m 1 9-year-old boy

Sensitive portrayal of a family in the midst of a divorce: mother
and father each wanting custody of their son. Sexually explicit
language.

Leona: early 30s, [lead], painter, avant garde, career on
    the rise, loving mother, hurt, torn, angry, feeling pres-
    sures of single parenthood.
Annie: mid 50s, [short role], neighbor, friend, landlady,
    down-to-earth, outspoken, merry widow, motherly, suppor-
    tive.

JEAN BRODIE see **THE PRIME OF MISS JEAN BRODIE**

JESSIE AND THE BANDIT QUEEN, David Freeman (1976)   Samuel French
1w 1m

Belle Starr and Jessie James act out the story of their lives and
their relationship in the days of the old west.

Belle Starr: 30, [lead], includes flashbacks to when she was
    17, strong, forceful, experienced in the ways of the
    world, tough with a vulnerable side, plays the piano.

JOE EGG, Peter Nicols (1967)   Samuel French
3w 3m   1 10-year-old girl

A couple conflicts on the issue of how to care for Jo, their 10-
year-old severely retarded daughter. Comedy.

Sheila: 30s, [lead], mothers everything: plants, animals,
    "vegetable" daughter, acts in community theater, jokes to
    lighten her family situation.
Pam: 30s, [supporting role], friend of Sheila, blasé affec-
    tations, fashionable, dislikes anything not beautiful.
Grace: 60s, [supporting role], suburban, fastidious, dresses
    in frills, Jo's grandmother.
Jo: 10, [supporting role], retarded daughter, makes sounds
    but not able to speak, can't walk or control arms.

JOSEPHINE: THE MOUSE SINGER, Michael McClure (1980)

Dram. Pl. Ser.

6-7w   6-7m

Fantasy about a singing mouse who wishes to be free of the neces-
sity to work so she can devote herself to her art and her hard
working tribe ambivalent about the value of her music. Comedy-
verse.

> Josephine: teens-early 20s, [lead], artistic, self centered,
>   intense, arrogant.
> Narrator: [supporting role], could be either gender.
> Sycophant One: any age, [short role], admirer and supporter
>   of Josephine.
> Mother Mouse: 30-40s, [short role].
> Mouse A, B, C, D, & E: [short roles], townsfolk.
> Mouse ghosts: [short roles].

THE KILLING OF SISTER GEORGE, Frank Marcus (1965)   Samuel French
4w

Repercussions in the life of a TV soap opera star when news comes
that her character is to be written out of the series.

> June: 40-50s, [lead], heavy-set, plays kind do-gooder on TV
>   show, in real life smokes cigars, uses generous amounts
>   of profanity, drinks gin, and temperamentally dominates
>   her lesbian lover.
> Alice: 30s, [lead], young looking, June's lover, waits on
>   June hand and foot.
> Mrs. Mercy Croft: 30-50s, [supporting role], indeterminate
>   age, business like assistant head at BBC radio.
> Madam Xenia: 60-70s, [supporting role], fortune teller,
>   exotic dress, beads.

KILLINGS ON THE LAST LINE, Lavone Mueller (1980)   Samuel French
                    or American Place Theater Women's Project
9w 1m

Angry treatise on poor conditions and oppression of workers in a
reactor parts factory. Black roles. Sexually explicit.

> Starkey: 19, [supporting role], wants to improve her job
>   opportunities and is studying technical materials.
> Mrs. Starkey: 51, [supporting role], defiant, kookie mother
>   of Starkey.
> Hidelman: 32, [supporting role], angry, outspoken, strong,
>   muscular.
> Ellis: 30, [supporting role], from Kentucky, sneaks her baby
>   in at work because she doesn't have anybody to care for
>   it at home.
> Juba: 45, [supporting role], Bahamian, sings song in play.
> Quashie: 44, [supporting role], Bahamian, has leg in cast.

Betty: 60, [supporting role], factory worker, widow.
Mavis: 35, [supporting role], union representative, company
    sympathizer.
Day Tripper: 75, [short role], part-time maintenance worker.

THE KNIGHT AT THE TWELFTH SAUCER, Marc Alan Zagoren (1977)
                              Chilton Book Co. or Best Short Plays 77
3w 1m

Two women scheme to encourage a marriage match between their
adult children pushing them reluctantly into a dinner meeting.
Comedy. Short play.

Rose: 40-50s, [supporting role], overweight, large, obsessed
    with food, still manages to be delicate.
Tillie: 40-50s, [supporting role], tired, frail.
Shanakind: 24, [supporting role], large and overweight,
    unkempt, spoiled, gluttonous.

LADIES AT THE ALAMO, Paul Zindel (1977)   Dram. Pl. Ser.
5w

The multi-million-dollar Alamo Theater is the setting for a
conflict between its chairperson and its artistic director.

Dede Cooper: 40s, [lead], charming, gutsy, intense, indi-
    vidualist.
Bella Gardner: 40s, [lead], calculating, heavy drinker,
    small time star, expensively dressed.
Suits: 20-30s, [supporting role], jolly, fat, undercurrent
    of power.
Joanne Remington: 40s, [supporting role], powerful, rich,
    repressed aggressions.
Shirley Fuller: 30-40s, [supporting role], Academy Award
    nominee, very energetic, active.

THE LADIES SHOULD BE IN BED, Paul Zindel (1973)   Dram. Pl. Ser.
6w

A bridge game with four middle class matrons degenerates showing
their vile sides when they get involved with an alleged sexual
pervert in a building across the street.

Maggie: 40s, [lead], noisy, theatrical, vicious, bigot,
    drinking too many Manhattans.
Charlotte: 40s, [lead], teacher, plump, caustic, sexually
    explicit language, B'nai B'rith award winner.
Elinore: 45, [supporting role], unmarried, lives with elder-
    ly mother, hostess for the day.
Maureen: 40, [supporting role], nurse, stable influence,
    quiet, helpful, softer than others.

Lucille: over 40, [supporting role], [black], domestic ser-
    vant.
Old woman: 80s, [very short], feeble, Elinore's mother.

THE LADY FROM DUBUQUE, Edward Albee (1980)   Dram. Pl. Ser.
4w 4m

Strange visitors comfort a woman dying of cancer when her husband
and frivolous friends cannot handle the situation.

Jo: 30s, [lead],   sick and dying from cancer, realistic,
    angry.
Elizabeth: 40-50s, [supporting role], wise and mysterious
    stranger, angel of mercy who understands and supports Jo.
Lucinda: 30s [supporting role], friend, shallow, caustic.
Carol: 30s, [supporting role], friend, glamorous, not very
    bright.

LADY OF LARKSPUR LOTION, Tennessee Williams (1945) Dram Pl. Ser.
2w 1m

An encounter between a realistic landlady trying to collect the
rent and her alcoholic derelict tenant who lives in a grand world
of illusion. Short play.

Mrs. Hardwicke-Moore: 40s, [lead], peroxide blonde, prosti-
    tute with fantasies of elegance.
Mrs. Wire: 50s, [supporting role], blunt, unkempt, over-
    weight landlady.

LADYHOUSE BLUES, Kevin O'Morrison (1979)   Samuel French
5w

In August 1919 in South St. Louis, a mother and the sisters of a
soldier await his return.

Liz: 41, [supporting role], the mother, attractive with sex
    appeal, farm reared, plain, rustic, uneducated, Bible
    reading fundamentalist.

the sisters:
Helen: 24, [supporting role], beautiful blonde, ravaged by
    tuberculosis.
Dot: 21, [supporting role], chic, mature for age, married to
    wealthy, upper crust man, six months pregnant.
Terry: 18, [supporting role], "full of herself" exuberant,
    her own woman.
Eylie: 16, [supporting role], waitress, audacious, sexy.

THE LARK, Jean Anouilh, adapt. by Lillian Hellman (1953)
Dram. Pl. Ser.
5w 15m

The story of Joan of Arc: the French country girl and religious zealot who lead an army, crowned the king, was burned at the stake for heresy, and later canonized as a saint by the church.

> Joan: late teens, [lead], small, youthful, fanatical, brave, defiant and unbending.
> Joan's mother: late 30s-40s, [short role], loving, supportive.
> Little Queen: 20s, [short role], inept wife of Charles, nominal ruler of France, frivolous, sheltered.
> Agnes Sorel: 20s, [short role], mistress of Charles, fashionable, frivolous.
> Queen Yolande: 40s, [short role], mother of Little Queen, worldly, realistic.

THE LAST OF MRS. LINCOLN, James Prideaux (1973)   Dram. Pl. Ser.
5w 11m

The many tragedies which befell the president's widow after his assassination. (Julie Harris won best performance award for her portrayal of this role).

> Mary Todd Lincoln: 40-50s, [lead], compassionate and courageous in the face of a long series of tragic events.
> Mary Harlan: 20-30s, [lead], Mrs. Lincoln's daughter-in-law, kind, from wealthy family.
> Elizabeth Edwards: 50-60s, [supporting role], Mrs. Lincoln's sister, fusses over her, solicitous, concerned, proper.
> Mrs. McCullough: 50-60s, [supporting role], old friend of Mrs. Lincoln, talkative, trite, shallow.
> Lizzie Keckley: 40-50s, [supporting role], [black], former slave, spunky servant.

THE LAST OF THE RED HOT LOVERS, Neil Simon (1970)   Samuel French
3w 1m

A 47-year-old man who has been a faithful husband for 23 years wants to become sexually liberated and tries three times unsuccessfully to start up an affair. Comedy.

> Elaine: late 30s, [supporting role], sexy, direct, matter of fact about sex, moderately attractive, craves cigarettes.
> Bobbi: 27, [supporting role], nutty actress, nervous, pot smoking, fresh, pretty, frequently mixed up with weirdos.
> Jeanette: 39, [supporting role], gloomy, despairing, depressed, in analysis, taking pills, indifferent about sex.

A LATE SNOW, Jane Chambers (1974)   Gay Plays
5w

Ellie, a professor at a local college, finds herself snow bound in a lakeside cabin with her lesbian lover, a former lover, a former roommate, and a writer with whom she is forming a new relationship.

> Ellie: mid 30s, [lead], attractive, cool, career oriented, keeps her personal relationships private to avoid criticism.
> Quincy: mid 20s, [lead], open, honest, a writer, present lover of Ellie, impatient with having to hide her relationship with Ellie.
> Pat: mid 30s, [lead], attractive, witty, holds no punches, self-assured antique dealer, alcoholic, Ellie's former lover.
> Margo: 40s, [supporting role], well-known writer, has been living as a recluse, self contained, attractive, warm, talented, charming.
> Peggy: mid 30s, [supporting role], suburban housewife, tries to do everything right, former roommate of Ellie, conventional, fashionable.

LATER, Corinne Jacker (1978)   Dram. Pl. Ser.
3w

A newly widowed woman and her two adult daughters evaluate their lives while at their Rhode Island sea-side home.

> Molly: late 50s, [lead], in mourning for husband, edgy, has ulcer, well educated, literate, former teacher, progressive.
> Kate: late 30s-early 40s, [lead], older daughter, bossy, stubborn, argumentative, unpredictable, thorny, manipulative.
> Laurie: late 30s, [lead], younger daughter, married, mother of two adolescent boys, softer.

LEMONADE, James Prideaux (1969)   Dram. Pl. Ser.
2w

Two matronly well-to-do women converse, quarrel, and make up as they sell spiked lemonade along the highway. Short play.

> Mabel: 50s, [lead], affluent, expensively dressed.
> Edith: 50s, [lead], slightly younger, a little smaller than Mabel, also affluent.

LET ME HEAR YOU SMILE, Leonora Thuna, Harry Cauley (1971)
Samuel French
1w 2m

Hannah relives her life, love, and marriage from her present age
of 70, back to her late 30s, and then to when she was six.
Comedy.

> Hannah: 70, [lead], homebody kindergarten teacher whose
>   husband has just retired.

LET ME HEAR YOU WHISPER, Paul Zindel (1970)   Dram. Pl. Ser.
5w 1 dolphin (puppet)

Helen is determined to save a dolphin she has befriended which is
scheduled for brain dissection. Short play. note: there is
another version of this play which calls for three of the roles
to be played by male actors.

> Helen: 50-60s, [lead], cleaning lady in laboratory, feeds
>   stray cats and dogs, tender hearted.
> Miss Moray: 40-50s, [lead], uptight, brisk, efficient, mean,
>   Helen's supervisor.
> Dr. Crocus: 30-60s, [short role], unkind scientist who per-
>   forms weird experiments on animals.
> Ms. Fridge: 30-60s, [short role], assistant, not very
>   bright, obedient and loyal to Crocus.
> Danielle: 20-40s, [supporting role], talky janitor, easy-
>   going, irresponsible.

LETTERS HOME, Rose Leiman Goldemberg (1979)   Samuel French
2w

Based on letters the gifted poet Sylvia Plath sent her mother
from her first days at Smith College in 1950, through marriage
and family in London, to her suicide in 1963.

> Sylvia: 20-30s, [lead], sensitive artist, writer, unhappy.
> Aurelia: late 40s-50s, [lead], Sylvia's mother, loving sup-
>   portive.

LOOK AWAY, Jerome Kilty (1973)   Samuel French
2w

As she is about to leave the insane asylum, the widow of President Lincoln discusses with her dressmaker the joys, sorrows, and
bitterness of her past experiences. Black part.

> Mary Todd Lincoln: 50s, [lead], embittered by a life full of
>   tragedies.

Elizabeth Keckley: 40-50s, [lead], [black], dressmaker, had
    been a slave and bought her freedom, spirited, indomita-
    ble.

LOOK: WE'VE COME THROUGH, Hugh Wheeler (1961)
                                    <u>Broadway's</u> <u>Beautiful</u> <u>Losers</u>
2w 4m

Two ordinary people surrounded by thoughtless opportunists take
solace in each other's company.

Belle Dort: 19, [lead], plain, wears glasses, highly intel-
    ligent book worm, works for publishing house, idealistic,
    kind, big hearted, self negating.
Jennifer Lewison: 21, [supporting role], struggling thespian,
    vain, pretty, slick, tries to be sophisticated.

LOOSE ENDS, Michael Weller (1979)   Samuel French
4w 5m

The marriage between a professional photographer and a film maker
becomes stressed over the issue of whether or not to have children. Asian role.

Susan: 20-30s, [lead], rising professional photographer,
    talented, wants to avoid personal commitment, doesn't
    want children.
Maraya: 30s, [supporting role], maternal, earthy, domestic,
    several pregnancies during course of play.
Selina: 30s, [supporting role], Chinese-American, film mak-
    er, steady and well balanced, works with Susan's husband.
Janice: 30s, [supporting role], friend of Susan.

A LOVELY SUNDAY FOR CREVE COEUR, Tennessee Williams (1978)
                                            Dram. Pl. Ser.
4w

In St. Louis in the 1930s, Dorothea is torn between Bodey who
wants her to marry and Helena who believes she should improve her
social position in life.

Dorothea: 30s, [lead], romantic dreamer, fading Southern
    belle, waiting for man to call, and hoping for proposal.
Bodey: 40s, [lead], short, plump, simple, common, unedu-
    cated, German accent, hard-of-hearing.
Helena: 30s, [lead], stylish, elegant, arrogant, snobbish
    affectations.
Miss Gluck: 50-60s, [short role], humorous, German speaking.

LOVERS, Brian Friel (1968)   Farrar, Straus, & Giroux
5w 2m

Two short plays set in Northern Ireland.

Winners- the idyllic romance of young lovers who will soon meet a
tragic end.

>   Mag: 17, [lead], vivacious, full of life and enthusiasm for
>   the future.
>   The Woman: 50s, [supporting role], impersonal commentator,
>   sits to the side on a stool and observes action.

Losers- the conflicts and pressures of an unhappy middle-aged
married couple.

>   Hanna: late 40s, [supporting role], caught between her hus-
>   band and her live-in mother's dominance.
>   Mrs. Wilson: 60s, [supporting role], Hanna's invalid mother,
>   domineering, uses her sickness to manipulate family.
>   Cissy: late 60s, [supporting role], next door neighbor,
>   friend of Mrs. Wilson, small, frail.

LOVERS AND OTHER STRANGERS, Renee Taylor, Joseph Bologna, (1968)
                                                    Samuel French
5w

Five short plays with the theme of humor in marriage. Comedy.

Brenda and Jerry, A comic first meeting and sexual encounter.

>   Brenda: early 20s, [lead], mod, attractive, glib, defensive
>   facade.

Hal and Cathy, A woman gets fed up with her affair with a married man who keeps promising to leave his wife someday, but never
does.

>   Cathy: 20s-30s, [lead], soft touch, silly, comic.

Johnny and Wilma, A married couple has an argument in bed.

>   Wilma: late 30s, [lead], strong, attractive, searching for
>   sexual identity, sexually assertive.

Mike and Susan, A man filled with anxiety about his wedding
scheduled for the next day runs over to his fiancee's apartment
at 4 am to talk about his doubts and fears.

>   Susan: 20s, [short role], sweet, kind, understanding,
>   placid, unperturbed.

<u>Bea</u>, <u>Frank</u>, <u>Richie</u> <u>and</u> <u>Joan</u>, A man having marital difficulties
goes to his parents for advice.

> Bea: 40-50s, [supporting role], son having disagreement with
> his wife, old fashioned, stubborn, intolerant.
> Joan: 20s, [supporting role], Bea's daughter-in-law, roman-
> tic, feels she is the injured party in marital dispute.

THE LOVES OF CASS MCGUIRE, Brian Friel (1966)   Samuel French
4w 6m

Cass returns to her brother's family in Ireland after 52 years of
working in American saloons only to be farmed out to a nursing
home where she lives in her memories.

> Cass: 70, [lead], tall, gaudily dressed, chain smoker, vul-
> gar, has more humanity than those around her, feels iso-
> lated.
> Alice: 50s, [short role], sister-in-law of Cass, expensively
> dressed.
> Tessa: 18, [short role], outspoken, cheeky maid.
> Mrs. Butcher: 80s, [short role], new resident of nursing
> home.
> Mother: 89, [short role], in wheelchair.

LU ANN HAMPTON LAVERTY OBERLANDER, Preston Jones (1976)
3w 8m   Dram. Pl. Ser.

Twenty years in the unhappy life of a former high school beauty
queen.

> LuAnn: [lead], first act: wholesome high school cheerlead-
> er, attractive, good figure; second act: 10 years later,
> hardened beauty operator; third act: another 10 years
> later, matronly beautiful, coarse, lively, works for
> the welcome wagon.
> Charmaine: teen, [supporting role], sassy, argumentative,
> jeering daughter of LuAnn.
> Claudine; 40s, [supporting role], stout, greyish blonde
> hair, widowed mother of LuAnn, complains, in last act
> she appears paralyzed in a wheel chair.

LUDLOW FAIR, Lanford Wilson (1965)   Dram. Pl. Ser.
2w

Rachel has regrets after she turned her boyfriend into the police
for stealing from her, and her roommate Agnes tries to cheer her
up.

> Rachel: [lead], 20-30s, dramatic, fast-living, glamorous.
> Agnes: [lead], 20-30s, shy, plain, joking, kooky.

LUNCH HOUR, Jean Kerr (1980)   Samuel French
2w 3m

Witty comedy about a woman and a man who decide to retaliate in
kind when they learn that their spouses are having an affair.

> Carrie: [lead], 23, slender, pretty, kookie, disorganized,
>   clumsy, self-depreciating, scatter-brained, invents re-
>   taliatory affair.
> Nora: [lead], early 30s, very attractive, dressed impec-
>   cably, clever, well-organized, having affair that creates
>   the situation.

LUNCH OR SOMETHING, Elizabeth Gray (1980)   Samuel French
2w + chorus of women

A play about facades where characters wear masques which they
remove when speaking the truth. Two old friends who were both in
love with the same man flashback to incidents in their lives together. Short play.

> Pam: [lead], 20s, sophisticated, educated.
> Janet: [lead], late 20s, sophisticated, educated, well
>   dressed.

THE MADWOMAN OF CHAILLOT, Jean Anouilh (1947)   Dram. Pl. Ser.
8w 17m (doubling)

Delightful tale of an eccentric countess who saves Paris from
evil men who are planning to dig up Paris in search of oil.
Fantasy.

> Countess Aurelia: [lead], 60s, indomitable optimist, loves
>   life, wildly eccentric, clever.
> Mme. Constance: [supporting role], 60s, madwoman of Passy,
>   dressed all in white, elaborate, dainty, large hat with
>   ostrich plumes.
> Mlle. Gabrielle: [supporting role], 60s, madwoman of St.
>   Sulpice, outdated dress, overdone makeup, coy, has imag-
>   inary dog following her.
> Mme. Josephine: [supporting role], 60s, madwoman of La Con-
>   corde, fantastically dressed, out of touch with reality,
>   but very practical, majestic.
> Irma: [short role], 20, angelic, waitress, only person who
>   understands deaf mute.
> Flower girl: [short role], teen, sells flowers.
> 3 women: [very short roles], any age, artificial, erect,
>   soul-less.

THE MAIDS, Jean Genet (1954)   Samuel French
3w

Two venomous servant girls take turns pretending to be the lady
of the manor, dressing up, putting on airs; and plotting to murder their employer.

> Solange: early 30s, [lead], older sister, angry, bitter,
>   jealous of woman she works for.
> Claire: early 30s, [lead], younger sister, vengeful, hateful
>   and frustrated.
> Madam: late 20s, [supporting role], wealthy, dramatically
>   gloomy, husband has been sentenced to prison.

MAJOR BARBARA, George Bernard Shaw (1905)   Samuel French
6w 9m

Major Barbara devoted to the cause of saving souls through the
Salvation Army is reunited with her long lost father the owner of
a munitions factory, and finds much to debate. Comedy.

> Barbara Undershaft: early 20s, [lead], intelligent, intense-
>   ly committed to her cause, energetic, hearty.
> Lady Britomart: 50s, [supporting role], mother of Barbara,
>   brusque, independent, liberal thinker.
> Sarah Undershaft: early 20s, [short role], younger sister of
>   Barbara, fashionable, slim, mundane.
> Jenny Hill: 18, [supporting role], pale, pretty, Salvation
>   Army worker, overwrought, pious.
> Rummy Mitchens: "looks 60, but probably 45," [short role],
>   old, worn out, in rags, common.
> Mrs. Baines: 40s, [short role], Salvation Army Commissioner,
>   earnest, appealing.

A MATTER OF GRAVITY, Enid Bagnold (1968)   Samuel French
4w 4m

An aging, aristocratic, English woman with liberal leanings deals
with economic pressures to sell her decaying estate, and is
reminded that times are changing during a visit from her grand-
son, a Socialist Oxford student. Originally titled <u>Call</u> <u>Me</u> <u>Jacky</u>.

> Mrs. Basil: 60s, [lead], grandmother, young for her age,
>   gallant, very upper class, open, frank, realistic, trying
>   to be flexible.
> DuBois: 20s, [supporting role], all purpose servant, short
>   hair, filled with inner conflict, gloomy, looking for
>   love and approval from Mrs Basil, drinks wine all day,
>   suspected lesbian.
> Shatov: 18-25, [supporting role], political leftist, activ-
>   ist, against the system, dominant in lesbian relationship
>   with Elizabeth.

Elizabeth: 18-25, [supporting role], softer, more traditional, raised in Trinidad, loves old English ways, respects
wealth and power, outspoken.

MAUD GONNE SAYS NO TO THE POET, Susan Rivers (1978)
author or   West Coast Plays #3
2w 1m

Inventive play-within-a-play and character study of a colorful
performer showing her relationships with her lover and with her
daughter. Short play.

Maud: 50, [lead], colorful, extravagant, articulate, maud-
lin, given to Gaelic excesses, fabricates and colors her
memories, plays violin.
Izzie: 30s, [supporting role], Maud's daughter, practical,
serious, sober.

A MEMBER OF THE WEDDING, Carson McCullers (1951)   Dram. Pl. Ser.
7w 6m 1 7-year-old boy

An adolescent Georgia girl, unsure of herself, goes through
heartbreaks and growing pains. Black roles.

Berenice Sadie Brown: 45, [lead], [black], cook, heavy-set,
loving, wise, motherly.
Frankie: 12, [lead], awkward, gangling, boyish, unhappy,
feels like a misfit, and inadequate.
Janice: 19, [short role], pretty but ordinary.
Mrs. West: 33, [short role], vivacious, blonde hair, dowdily
dressed.
Doris: 14, [bit part], pretty, popular, happy.
Helen: 14, [bit part], pretty, popular, happy.
Sis Laura: [bit part], [black], very old woman.

MEMOIR, John Murrell (1977)   Plays of the Year vol. 48
or Granada Publishing
1w 1m

Renown performer and producer, the legendary Sarah Bernhardt, a
year before her death, is writing her second autobiography with
the help of a male secretary.

Sarah Bernhardt: 77, [lead], grandiose, romantic, enchant-
ing, temperamental, fiercely independent, has one leg
amputated.

MIDNIGHT CALLER, Horton Foote (1956)   Dram. Pl. Ser.
5w 2m

An unhappy woman in a small town moves into a boarding house and falls in love with a new boarder. Short play.

> Helen: 28, [lead], strong, sensible, warm, compassionate.
> Alma Jean: 38, [lead], haughty, prim, hard to please, com-
> plaining, works in court house.
> Cutie: 28, [supporting role], tolerant, softer, hard work-
> ing, sensitive.
> Miss Rowena: 60s, [supporting role], coy Southern belle,
> romantic, school teacher.
> Mrs. Crawford: 50s, [supporting role], proprietor of board-
> ing house, motherly.

MILDRED WILD see **THE SECRET AFFAIRS OF MILDRED WILD**

MIMOSA PUDICA, Curt Dempster (1974)   Lois Berman
                                        or Best Short Plays 77
1w 1m

A couple of lonely apartment building neighbors cheer each other
up on Christmas Eve. Short play.

> Dianne: 25, [lead], Italian descent, friendly, vivacious,
> plain but attractive.

THE MIRACLE WORKER, William Gibson (1956)   Samuel French
7w 5m   6 girls-bit parts

The story of the work of Annie Sullivan, which changed Hellen
Keller from a wild, unkempt, animal-like child into a gifted, intelligent young woman.

> Annie Sullivan: 20, [lead], tough Yankee, visually impaired,
> strong-willed, survivor of horrendous childhood growing
> up in institutions.
> Helen Keller: 6 1/2, [lead], wild, undisciplined, blind and
> deaf, unable to talk or communicate, unrestrained, sub-
> ject to extreme frustration, easily flies into rages.
> Kate Keller: late 20s-early 30s, [supporting role], Helen's
> mother, sweet, girlish, tender hearted, loving, gentle,
> unable to cope with Helen.
> Aunt Ev: over 35, [short role], loving, supportive, proper,
> strong family pride.
> Viney: any age, [short role], [black], servant.
> Martha: 6-8, [short role], [black], neighbor child.

MISS JEAN BRODIE, See **THE PRIME OF MISS JEAN BRODIE**

MISS MARGARIDA'S WAY, Roberto Athayde (1978)   Samuel French
1w 1m (non speaking)

In an allegorical treatment, a school teacher harangues and badgers her class, which is the audience.

> Miss Margarida: 30-50s, [lead], a prototype of a totalitarian dictator in the person of an eighth grade biology teacher.

MISS REARDON DRINKS A LITTLE, See **AND MISS REARDON DRINKS A LITTLE**

MOJO, Alice Childress (1971)   Dram. Pl. Ser.
1w 1m

A love story concerning a formerly married couple set against a backdrop of civil rights demonstrations. The woman has learned that she has cancer. Black cast. Short play.

> Irene: 30 plus, [lead], angry, but loving, has life-threatening cancer.

A MOON FOR THE MISBEGOTTEN, Eugene O'Neil (1945)   Samuel French
1w 4m

A ramshackle New England farm is the setting for an encounter between Josie, a big, strong farm woman, and James Tyrone, a self-destructive, heavy drinking New York playboy.

> Josie: late 20s, [lead], powerful, large and strong, but still feminine, Irish looking with thick black hair and fair skin.

MORNINGS AT SEVEN, Paul Osborn (1939)   Samuel French
5w 4m

Gentle romance of Myrtle and Homer who have been postponing marriage for 15 years, and the relationships of Homer's mother and aunts.

> Myrtle: 30s, [supporting role], Homer's fiancee, sweet, gushy, wishy-washy.
> Esther 72, [supporting role], Homer's aunt, cheerful, once a beauty, fun loving, has demanding husband.
> Cora: 70, [supporting role], Homer's aunt, easy going, shares her home with sister, Aaronetta, but would rather live separately, jealous of Aaronetta.
> Ida: 66, [supporting role], Homer's mother, reluctant to let him go, husband has spells.

Aaronetta: 60s,   [supporting role], Homer's aunt, independent, never married, in love with Cora's husband.

MR. BIGGS, Anna Marie Barlow, (1964)   New American Plays vol. 1
2w 1m

Two eccentric elderly sisters living together in an elegant Vic-
torian house disagree on the unusual attachment one of them has
for a former roomer. Horror story. Short play.

Eloise: over 70, [lead], realistic, stronger of the two,
kind, gentle.
Mary: over 70, [lead], sentimental, clinging, frightened,
sensitive.

MRS. DALLY HAS A LOVER, William Hanley (1962)   Dram. Pl. Ser.
1w 1m

A romance between an older woman and a younger man.

Mrs. Dally: late 30s, [lead], attractive, passionate, art-
tistic, poetic, living with a husband who doesn't understand her.

MY COUSIN RACHEL, Daphne DuMaurier, (1980)   Dram. Pl. Ser.
adapted by Diana Morgan
2w 5m

The Italian widow of Phillip's deceased uncle ignites a wave of
suspicions when Phillip falls madly in love with her and gives
the family estate to her. Gothic drama.

Rachel: 35, [lead], beautiful, beguiling, mysterious, clever, self-centered, materialistic, loves the fine things
in life.
Louise: 18, [supporting role], innocent, well-to-do, pretty,
idealistic.

MY CUP RANNETH OVER, Robert Patrick (1978)   Dram. Pl. Ser.
                                          or Best Short Plays 80
2w

A punk folk-rock singer is hit with sudden success and her writer
roommate gets jealous. Short play.

Paula: mid 20s, [lead], unpublished writer, attractive,
trim, smug, dominant half of pair.
Yucca: mid 20s, [lead], singer, easy going, scrawny, tousled
hair, stained T shirt.

MY SISTER IN THIS HOUSE, Wendy Kesselman (1982)   Samuel French
4w (3m, off stage voices)

In Paris 1933 two cruelly oppressed servants reach a breaking
point, and in a violent outburst, murder their employer and her
daughter.

> Christine: early 20s, [lead], servant, assured, neat, quick,
> talented in needlework, protective of sister.
> Lea: teens, [lead], servant, younger sister, timid, in-
> secure, new to household, raised in convent, clumsy.
> Madame Danzard: early 50s, [lead], stingy employer, domi-
> neering, petty, questionable taste in clothes, cruel.
> Isabelle Danzard: early 20s, [supporting role], inept
> daughter, dependent, constrained, down trodden.

NEVIS MOUNTAIN DEW, Steve Carter (1978)   Dram. Pl. Ser.
3w 4m

A helpless invalid in an iron lung asks to have his life ended so
his family will not have to make sacrifices for him anymore.
Black cast.

> Everelda: 49, [supporting role], sister, reserved, sour,
> dresses too old for her age, righteous, self sacrificing,
> broke up with her husband a long time ago.
> Zepora: 43, [supporting role], sister, lively, fun loving,
> kind, drinks.
> Billie: 40s, [supporting role], wife, good looking, loyal to
> incapacitated husband, feels responsible for his condi-
> tion.

'NIGHT MOTHER, Marsha Norman, (1983)   Hill and Wang
2w

Frightening conversation in which a daughter announces to her
mother with unnerving certainty that she intends to kill herself
that evening and devastatingly reveals the emptiness and futility of her life.

> Thelma: 50s-60s, [lead], mother, ordinary, conventional,
> talkative, recently widowed.
> Jessie: 30s, [lead], daughter, overweight, total lack of
> self esteem, clear determination.

NIGHT THOUGHTS, Corinne Jacker (1977)   Dram. Pl. Ser.
2w

Relationship between two older women, one very ill and connected
to a life sustaining machine. Absurdist comedy.

Dorothy: 60-70s, [lead], weak, chronic invalid, lonely,
   difficult to get along with, fabricates reality, suspicious.
Ida: 60s, [lead], healthy, energetic, tries to encourage
   Dorothy.

NORMAN CONQUESTS, Allan Ayckbourn (1975)   Samuel French
3w 3m

The theme of Norman attempting to seduce three different women
carries through three plays with the same cast of characters:
Table Manners, Living Together, and Round and Round the Garden.

Annie: 20-30s, [supporting role], attractive, but careless
   and casual about grooming, sloppy.
Sarah: 30s, [supporting role], Annie's sister-in-law, inter-
   fering, proper and righteous.
Ruth: 30s, [supporting role], older sister of Annie, wife
   of Norman, crisp, cool, realistic, worldly, poor vision,
   but won't wear glasses.

NUTS, Tom Topor (1980)   Samuel French
3w 6m

A woman accused of murder struggles to prove her sanity in order
that she may stand trial for a murder she committed in self de-
fense; speaks out eloquently against the system.

Claudia: early 30s, [lead], outspoken, intelligent, being
   kept in mental ward, had been prostitute.
Rose: late 50s, [supporting role], Claudia's mother, worries
   about her daughter.
Recorder: [very short role], court worker.

**OH DAD, POOR DAD, MAMMA'S HUNG YOU IN THE CLOSET AND I'M FEELING
   SO SAD,** Arthur L. Kopit (1959)   Samuel French
2w 4m

Farcical parody about a macabre, tyrannical woman and her timid,
over-protected 17-year-old son.

Madame Rosepettle: 50s, [lead], overpowering, paranoid,
   warped, acid, puritanical about sex.
Rosalie: 19, [supporting role], robust, lively, lusty, se-
   ductive.

OLD TIMES, Harold Pinter (1971)   Dram. Pl. Ser.
2w 1m

In their house by the sea, Kate and her movie-maker husband are

visited by an old roommate of Kate and spend the evening remi-
niscing.

>   Kate: early 40s, [lead], quiet, introvert, dreamer.
>   Anna: early 40s, [lead], outgoing, friendly, gregarious,
>   former roommate of Kate.

ON GOLDEN POND, Ernest Thompson (1979)   Dram. Pl. Ser.
2w 4m 1 13-year-old boy

At the family summer home a grouchy, intolerant, elderly man
struggles through personal relationships during a visit by his
daughter and a 13-year-old boy.

>   Ethel Thayer: 69, [lead], small, energetic, strong, smoothes
>   over Norman's irritability and irascibility.
>   Chelsea: 30-40s, [supporting role], daughter, high strung,
>   resentful, unresolved in her relationship with her fa-
>   ther.

ONCE A CATHOLIC, Mary O'Malley (1978)   Samuel French
10w 4m

The stresses, pressures, and problems of the students in a
London convent girls' school showing their survival methods.
Comedy.

>   Mother Peter: 40-50s, [supporting role], nun, tall, stout,
>   venomous teacher.
>   Mother Basil: 60s-70s, [supporting role], nun, short, fat,
>   nags students.
>   Mother Thomas Aquinas: 20s-30s, [supporting role], tall,
>   thin, refined, head teacher, venomous.
>   Mary Mooney: 15, [lead], plain, freckled, good singing
>   voice, from poor family.
>   Mary McGinty: 15, [supporting role], pretty, blonde, frivo-
>   lous.
>   Mary Gallagher: 15, [supporting role], attractive, sensible,
>   dark hair.
>   Mary O'Grady: 15, [short role], pretty.
>   Mary O'Hennessy: 15, [short role], fat.
>   Mary Flanagan: 15, [short role], brainy.
>   Mary Murphy: 15, [short role], small.

OPAL SERIES, John Patrick, Comedy-farce.   Dram. Pl. Ser.

Regulars in each play: (additional roles for particular plays
listed below)

>   Opal: 40s-50s, our beloved heroine, who innocently sails
>   through life unharmed by the evil doers who attempt to
>   take advantage of her. Zany, optimistic, raunchy, coarse

and   common,   she lives in a shack next to the city   dump
and collects junk.
Rosie: late 40s-50s, Opal's side-kick and best friend, caustic, bitter, husband left her 10 years ago.

EVERYBODY LOVES OPAL, (1961)
2w 4m

A sinister trio plotting to murder Opal makes several   ludicrous,
unsuccessful attempts.

Gloria: 19, [supporting role], brash, hard, mean, plotting
against Opal, over-done dress and make-up.

OPAL IS A DIAMOND, (1971)
3w   8m

Opal is   threatened by an unscrupulous politician and   finds   it
necessary to run against him in an election.

Mary: early 20s, [supporting role],   pretty,   self-assured
campaign assistant.

OPAL'S BABY, (1974)
4w 2m

This time the threat comes from some misinformed opportunists who
believe Opal is secretly wealthy and plot to get her money.

Verna: 20s, [supporting role],   shabby,   forlorn,   dirty,
timid, pretending to be pregnant to deceive Opal.
Granny: 60-80s, [supporting role], tiny, wild-eyed, crazy,
member of   gang of hoodlums trying to take advantage of
Opal.

OPAL'S HUSBAND, (1974)
3w 2m

Opal marries a 95-year-old man whose daughter is plotting against
him.

Velma: 40-60s, [supporting role],   daughter,   mean, large,
aggressive.

OPAL'S MILLION DOLLAR DUCK, (1979)
3w 1m

A pair of wicked actors attempt to trick Opal into selling them
what they believe is a valuable painting.

Queenie: 40-50s, [supporting role], flamboyant, faded blonde hair, pretentious, snobbish, greedy, underhanded.

OPENING NIGHT, John Cromwell (1968)   Chilton Book Co.
                                                       or Best Short Plays 68
2w

An alcoholic performer on the wagon struggles with temptation when a bottle of brandy from an admirer arrives on opening night. Short play.

Fanny Ellis: 50s-60s, [lead], clever, potent star, tough trouper, survivor, alcoholic.
Hecky: 60s, [supporting role], maid, companion and expert dresser, loving but firm.

OUT OF OUR FATHER'S HOUSE,   Paula Wagner, Jack Hosfsiss, Eve
    Merriam (1975) based on Growing Up Female in America: Ten
    Lives by Eve Merriam   Samuel French
3w (doubling)

Outstanding women from the 19th century describe the limitations placed upon women in that era and demonstrate unique attempts to circumnavigate them. Music added.

Elizabeth Cady Stanton: [lead], founder of women's suffrage movement.
Maria Mitchell: [lead], astronomer, intelligent, inventive, hungry for knowledge.
"Mother" Mary Jones: [lead], outspoken, committed, organizer of labor.
Dr. Anna Howard Shaw: medical doctor and minister.
Elizabeth Gertrude Stern: [lead], from the Jewish ghetto, career woman, writer.
Eliza Southgate: teens, [supporting role], schoolgirl, conventional, typical.

A PALM TREE IN A ROSE GARDEN, Meade Roberts (1955) Dram. Pl. Ser.
5w 3m

Movie buffs living in a typical Hollywood patio apartment building are headed by landlady, Rose, who once aspired to stardom, and now encourages other young women to go for it. References to movie stars of the 50s.

Rose Frobisher: early 50s, [lead], grandiose, enamored of Hollywood, plump, brightly dyed hair, loud jewelry, extravagantly dressed.
Lila: late 20s, [supporting role], Rose's daughter, looks older than her years, quiet, plain looking, intelligent, practical, not interested in movies.

Alice: late 30s, [supporting role], "small and wiry," tries
   unsuccessfully to be chic, movie buff.
Mona: 50s, [supporting role], large, heavy-set, neighbor in
   next building, friendly antagonism with Rose, used to
   work in films.
Barbara: late 20s, [supporting role], wants to be a star,
   works hard at having a beautiful image, ambitious, des-
   perate, insecure.

PATIO, Jack Heifner (1977)   Dram. Pl. Ser.
                                    or Best Short Plays 80
2w

Two small town sisters, one leaving for the big city and one a
perfectionist home body, prepare for a garden party. Short play.

Jewel: 30s, [lead], lots of jewelry, elaborate hair-do, easy
   going, calm.
Pearl: 30s, [lead], anxious hostess, wants her home to be
   perfect.

A PERFECT ANALYSIS GIVEN FOR A PARROT, Tennessee Williams (1958)
                                    Dram. Pl. Ser.
2w 1m   2 male extras

Two rollicking roguish conventioneers in Memphis, looking for a
party, get side tracked in a dumpy bar. Short play.

Bessie: 40s, [lead], heavy set, garishly dressed.
Flora: 40s, [lead], very thin, garishly dressed.

A PHOENIX TOO FREQUENT, Christopher Fry (1946)   Dram. Pl. Ser.
2w 1m

Set in ancient Roman times, a newly-widowed woman and her reluc-
tant maid withdraw from the world to mourn in his tomb. Their
resolve begins to fade when a handsome guard joins them. Comedy.
Short play.

Dynamene: 20-30s, [lead], beautiful, newly-widowed, filled
   with sorrow at her loss yet enjoying the drama of her
   situation.
Doto: 20-30s, [lead], servant, practical, earthy, thinking
   of her empty stomach.

PIZZA, Michelle Linfante (1980)   West Coast Plays #6
6w

Grace relives memories of her youth during the 50s: a family run
pizzeria in a tough Italian neighborhood in Patterson, N.J. and
her close, but neurotic relationship with her mother. Short play.

> Grace: 30s [lead], intelligent, creative, not pretty, ap-
>   pears as age 12, 15, and 20 during memory scenes.
> Lena: 50s [lead], mother of Grace, boisterous, generous,
>   superstitious, overprotective, possessive.
> Sadie: 50-60s, [supporting role], narrow minded busy-body,
>   friend of Lena.
> Perla: late teens-early 20s, [short role], new neighbor,
>   exotic dancer, flamboyantly dressed, Hispanic.
> Bonsey: teen, [short role], 50s style pin-ball-playing punk.
> Pizza lady: any age, [short role], delivers pizza.

PLEASE, NO FLOWERS, Joel Ensana (1969)   Chilton Book Co.
                                                     or Best Short Plays 69
6w 3m

Two dead women carry on a conversation from their caskets in a
funeral parlor as their friends and relatives come in to view
them. Short play.

> Lena Grosman: late 60s, [lead], now a ghost, was tired of
>   life.
> Esther Rubel: mid 30s, [lead], now a ghost, killed herself
>   jumping off Golden Gate Bridge.
> Mrs. Hirshman: 50s, [short role], wife of Esther's boss,
>   well dressed, heavy set, crabby.
> Mrs. Bleeker: 60s, [short role], fair-weather friend of
>   Lena.
> Mrs. Lehr: 60s, [short role], fair-weather friend of Lena.
> Sandy: 20s, [short role], attractive, kind, loving niece of
>   Lena.

PORCH, Jack Heifner (1976)   Dram. Pl. Ser.
                                                     or Best Short Plays 80
2w

Domineering mother and fearful daughter sit on front porch on a
hot summer evening as daughter struggles to break away from
mother's dominance. Short play.

> Dot: 70s, [lead], in wheelchair, controlling and clinging to
>   daughter, afraid to be left alone.
> Lucille: 40s, [lead], wearing old fashioned two-piece swim
>   suit, red hair, manipulated by mother.

THE PRIMARY ENGLISH CLASS, Israel Horowitz (1976)   Dram. Pl.Ser.
4w 5m

A comical picture of an English-as-Second-Language class in which
each pupil speaks a different language and no one can understand
anybody else. Calls for two Asian women parts, and Polish, Italian, French, and German-speaking men.

>   Debbie Westba: 20-30s, [lead], teacher, bright, competent.
>   Translator: any age, [supporting role], the person who com-
>   municates what the others are saying.
>   Yoko Kuzukago: 20s, [short role], Japanese-speaking, beauti-
>   ful, giggles a lot.
>   Mrs. Pong: elderly, [short role], Chinese-speaking.

THE PRIME OF MISS JEAN BRODIE, Muriel Sparks (1969) Samuel French
    adapted by Jay Presson Allen
15w 4m

At a Scottish girls' school in 1931 an independent, strong willed, charismatic school teacher, who inspires fierce loyalty among
her pupils, conflicts with the system.

>   Jean Brodie: 30-40s, [lead], powerful, heroic, prideful,
>   forceful, fanatically romantic, has progressive ideals.
>   Sandy: 11, 14, 16, (play spans 5 years and shows the stu-
>   dents at the ages mentioned), [lead], one of Brodie's
>   favorite pupils, very bright, adventurous, precocious,
>   works to gain Brodie's approval.
>   Monica: 11, 14, 16, [supporting role], talented in perform-
>   ing, outgoing, clowning.
>   Jenny: 11, 14, 16, [supporting role], favored pupil, very
>   pretty, graceful.
>   Mary: 11, 14, 16, [short role], slower student, timid, in-
>   ept, stutters.
>   Miss MacKay: 30-50s, [supporting role], headmistress, brisk,
>   no nonsense, conservative, angry, jealous of Brodie.
>   Sister Helena: 40s, [supporting role], pious cloistered nun,
>   author of acclaimed book, former student looking back.
>   Miss Campbell: [short role].
>   several short roles for students.

RAISIN IN THE SUN, Lorraine Hansberry (1959)   Samuel French
3w 6m   1 10-year-old boy

The struggles of a proud black family on Chicago's South side to
overcome limitations caused by racial oppression.

>   Lena Younger: early 60s, [lead], powerful matriarch, strong
>   authority, subtle beauty and grace, white hair, noble
>   carriage.
>   Beneatha: 20, [lead], Lena's daughter, lean, intellectual,
>   studying to become a doctor, has enthusiasm for life,

seeking identity.
Ruth: 30, [lead], Lena's daughter-in-law, mother of 10-year-
old son, weary, disappointed with life, once very pretty.

THE RATTLE OF A SIMPLE MAN, Charles Dyer (1963)   Samuel French
1w 2m

Moving love story of a prostitute who invents an aristocratic
family for herself and a lonely man who is clumsy and inexperi-
enced with women.

Cyrenne: 20-30s, [lead], intelligent, outspoken, poised,
beautiful, kind, haughty, mocking, tempestuous, fabricates stories about her life when she doesn't like reality.

REFLECTIONS IN A WINDOW, Beverley Byers Pevitts (1981)
Best Short Plays 82
9w 1m

Describes life in a nursing home and the pressures and conflicts
that occur in the families of the residents. Short play.

Bertie: 100, [supporting role], small, frail, spirited,
alert, plucky.
Alice: late 60s, [supporting role], Bertie's daughter,
quiet, friendly, loving.
Betty: early 30s, [supporting role], Bertie's granddaughter,
outgoing, stylishly casual, very much in charge.
Martha: 88, [supporting role], small, quiet, likable, loving
towards others.
Ruth: 72, [supporting role], strong willed, tries to walk
erect despite crippling arthritis.
Esther: 83, [supporting role], in wheelchair, wears lots of
jewelry, raspy voice.
Rebecca: 68, [supporting role], enormous body, too large to
walk, in wheelchair.
Margaret: 75, [short role], sad, unhappy, in wheelchair.

THE RIMERS OF ELDRITCH, Lanford Wilson (1966)   Dram. Pl. Ser.
10w 7m

Portrait of the prejudices and pressures in a small town in the
Bible Belt and the impact of a murder upon the residents.

Eva Jackson: 14, [supporting role], crippled, walks with
limp, unhappy, wistful, dreamy.
Evelyn Jackson: 30s, [supporting role], Eva's mother, mean,
nagging, overprotective, domineering, obsessed with
daughter's vulnerability.
Nelly Windrod: 40-50s, [supporting role], coarse, unpleas-
ant, bullies her elderly mother.

Mary Windrod: 60-70s, [supporting role], Nelly's mother,
    senile, wrapped up in memories, doesn't listen to people,
    obsessed with the town being evil.
Patsy Johnson: teen, [supporting role], pretty, stuck-up,
    flighty, doesn't like living in small town.
Mavis Johnson: 30-40s, [supporting role], Patsy's mother,
    indulgent towards Patsy.
Lena Truit: teen, [short role], friend of Patsy, sensible.
Martha Truit: 30-40s, [supporting role], Lena's mother,
    narrow minded gossip.
Wilma Atkins: 30-40s, [supporting role], Martha's friend,
    narrow minded gossip.
Cora Groves: 30-40s, [supporting role], owner of Hilltop
    Cafe, widow, has a young lover whom she indulges.

THE RIVER, James Elward (1965)   Dram. Pl. Ser.
3w 1m

Two women in a Greenwich Village cafe overhear a conversation in
the next booth between a young woman and an older man having an
affair. Short play.

Terry: 34, [lead], direct, positive outlook, broad hips and
    shoulders, but feminine.
Yvonne: 30, [lead], smaller than Terry, delicate, wistful,
    vulnerable, pretty.
The girl: early 20s, [supporting role], lonely, insecure,
    unhappy, attached to older man and bitter at his desire
    to withdraw.

THE ROADS TO HOME, Horton Foote (1982)   Dram. Pl. Ser.
3w 6m

Set in Houston, Texas in the twenties this story gives a gentle
treatment of the sad circumstances which lead to a young woman's
insanity.

Annie: late 20s-early 30s, [lead], delicate, dellusional,
    often out of touch with reality, unable to cope, has had
    many tragic experiences, has good singing voice.
Mabel: 42, [lead], friendly, warm, from small town, suppor-
    tive.
Vonnie: 40, [lead], Mabel's neighbor, kind, Southerner,
    friendly, folksy.

ROOM FOR ONE WOMAN, Samuel Shem (1979)   Best Short Plays 79
                                                 or Lois Berman
3w

Old woman fearful about leaving for nursing home tries to
persuade new tenant for her room to let her stay. Short play.

    Pedley: 75, [lead], uses two canes to walk, afraid of
       change, lives in the past.
    Besley: 60s, [lead], new tenant, cheerful, robust, but angry
       underneath.
    Lil: 40, [supporting role], overworked, impatient and re-
       sentful about the time she is spending to help Pedley
       move.

ROOMFUL OF ROSES, Edith Sommer (1954)   Dram. Pl. Ser.
5w 3m

Daughter of divorced couple leaves father's home to live with
mother after several years' separation. Cool, lonely, and defensive, she has difficulty accepting the love and warmth offered
her. Comedy drama.

    Bridget: 15, [lead], thin, vital, puts on affectations,
       hides her hurt feelings behind a facade.
    Nancy: 30s, [lead], attractive mother, generous, loving,
       vital, understanding.
    Jane: 15, [supporting role], bright, realistic, friend of
       Bridget.
    Grace: late 30s, [supporting role], mother of Jane, sympa-
       thetic, maternal, humorous, old friend of Nancy.
    Willamay: 30-50s, [short role], maid.

ROUGE ATOMIQUE, N. Richard Nash (1955)   Dram. Pl. Ser.
                                   or Best Short Plays 54
2w

In a casual distant manner two women wait for a phone call that
will report whether the man they both love will live or die.
Short play. Verse.

    Wife: 20-50s, [lead], angry possessive, fearful of losing
       husband.
    Woman: 20-50s, [lead], loving, attractive, believes man
       loves her more.

SAFE HOUSE, Nicholas Kazan (1977)   West Coast Plays #3
                                   or Susan Schulman
3w 2m

Carl, a former radical, now (1974) a psychiatrist practicing in
Berkeley, is asked to harbor two fugitives, members of the Weath-
er Underground, one of whom was a friend from student days. His
life and marriage are dramatically disrupted. Sexually explicit
language.

    Hillary: 29, [lead], militant radical, bombs buildings, is
       on FBI's most wanted list, sincerely committed to her
       cause, very self assured but human and vulnerable, styl-

ish dress, mod hat, bisexual.
Ruth: 28, [supporting role]), wife of Carl, pretty, had
    participated in student demonstrations but wants a con-
    ventional life.
Tink: 20s, [supporting role], Hillary's friend and sometimes
    lover, skinny, granny glasses, ascetic looking, off-beat,
    weird, sardonic.

SAME TIME NEXT YEAR, Bernard Slade (1975)   Samuel French
1w 1m

A couple meets for one weekend each year for 25 years. Each has
strong family commitments. Six scenes spaced five years apart re-
flect the changes in their lives. Comedy.

Doris: [lead], first scene late 20s, then five years older
    with each progressive scene up to her 50s in final scene.
    Changes from guilt-ridden, Catholic-reared girl, who
    didn't graduate from high school, to a hippie, then to a
    chic, successful business woman.

THE SAND CASTLE, Lanford Wilson (1967)   Dram. Pl. Ser.
3w 3m 1 12-year-old boy

A family whiles away their summer hours, and goes through growing
pain in a beach house near San Diego. Short play.

Irene: 40s, [supporting role], mother, "thin, quiet woman of
    considerable bearing", teaches at local college, widow.
Joan: 20s, [supporting role], Irene's daughter, playful
    college student.
Sasha: 20s, [supporting role], sexy, outgoing student.

SARAH AND THE SAX, Lewis John Carlino (1962)   Dram. Pl. Ser.
                                   or Two Short Plays
1w 1m

Touching chance meeting of a conventional older Jewish woman and
a black hip musician who overlook their differences because of
their common loneliness. Short play.

Sarah: 50s, [lead], cheerful, friendly, talkative, plump,
    traditional, lonely, husband and son both dead.

SAVE ME A PLACE AT FOREST LAWN, Lorees Yerby (1963)
                                        Dram. Pl. Ser.
2w

Two elderly women, best friends for many years, meet each day for
a meal at a cafeteria.

Clara: 80s, [lead], bossy, assertive, self-satisfied, knows
it all, but has a soft side.
Gertrude: 80s, [lead], fearful, emotional, but spunky, realistic.

THE SEA HORSE, Edward Moore (1969)   Samuel French
1w 1m

Love story between Gertrude, a proprietor of a waterfront bar on
the West Coast, and Harry, a seaman who wants to buy his own boat
and settle down.

Gertrude: late 30s, [lead], tired, grubby, overweight and
unusually tall, tough, and defensive because she's been
hurt in the past.

SEASCAPE, Edward Albee (1975)   Dram. Pl. Ser.
2w 2m

On an ocean beach a picnicking middle-aged couple encounter and
befriend two reptile-people who have emerged from the sea.

Nancy: 40-50s, [lead], friendly, enthusiastic, has a zest
for life.
Sarah: any age, [lead], a lizard-like reptile from the sea
who acts like a traditional 20th century human wife.

SECOND CHANCE, Elyse Nass (1979)   Best Short Plays 80
or Harold Freedman Brandt
2w

Dialogue between widowed woman who wants to get out and live life
fully and her friend who wants to play it safe and hide behind
her husband. Short play.

Rita: late 60s, [lead], widow, energetic, life loving, planning to perform in play wearing leotard and tights.
Evelyn: mid 60s, [lead], conservative friend who tries to
get Rita to slow down.

THE SECRET AFFAIRS OF MILDRED WILD, Paul Zindel (1973)
5w 4m   Dram. Pl. Ser.

Middle-aged proprietor of a candy store fantasizes herself in
scenes from 1930 movies, and a scene where she wins a TV contest.
Comedy.

Mildred: 40-50s, [lead], fanatic about movies, drably
dressed, but make-up and hair-do are bright and garish.
Berthe: 40-50s, [supporting role], energetic, landlady,
prudishly dressed, efficiency nut.

Helen: 50-60s, [supporting role], angry sister-in-law of
    Mildred.
Miss Manley: 20-40s, [supporting role], operates tape re-
    corder for TV publicity crew, slick, assertive, tough.
Sister Cecilia: any age, [short role], nun.

SEPARATE CEREMONIES, Phyllis Purscell (1981)   Am. Place Theater
4w 2m

Two sisters and a brother reunite for a family gathering at the
death of their father and realize his presence and influence is
still with them.

Carrie: early 40s, [lead], attractive, eldest child, respon-
    sible, surviving, cared for father during his illness,
    was with him at his death.
Addie: 30s, [lead], youngest child of family, tall, grace-
    ful, dancer living in San Francisco, humorous, outspoken,
    childish, defiant.
Lauren: 20s, [supporting role], daughter of Carrie, college
    student planning to take year off from school.
Grace: 70s, [supporting role], aunt, nurturing, likes to
    cook, traditional, remembers the old days.

SHOUT ACROSS THE RIVER, Stephen Poliakof (1979)   Methuen
2w 3m

A South London horror story of a deranged daughter who bullies
and brutalizes her insane mother.

Mrs. Forsythe: mid 30s, [lead], smartly dressed, good look-
    ing, nervous, insane.
Christine: 14, [lead], very quiet, sudden outbursts of vio-
    lence.

SISTER MARY IGNATIUS EXPLAINS IT ALL FOR YOU, Christopher Durang
    (1980)   Best Short Plays 81 or Dram. Pl. Ser.
3w 2m 1 boy

Biting satire on the results of an overly-dogmatic religious
education. Former pupils of Sister Mary Ignatius tell unsettling
tales of their present situations. Comedy.

Sister Mary Ignatius: 50s, [lead], dressed in old fashioned
    habit, mindlessly recites church doctrines, not very
    bright, ridiculous, out of touch.
Diane Symonds: 28-30, [supporting role], former pupil, sing-
    er, miserable, angry, has had three abortions.
Philomena Rostovitch: 28-30, [short role], former pupil,
    unwed mother.

6 RMS RIV VU, Bob Randall (1970)   Samuel French
4w 4m

A woman and a man (each married to someone else) are stranded
together in a vacant apartment, make love, but decide to call it
off and return to their respective spouses.

>   Anne: early 30s, [lead], witty, smart, wife and mother,
>   worries about whether or not she is hip.
>   Janet: early 30s, [supporting role], well-dressed, attrac-
>   tive, powerful, active in women's movement.
>   Woman in 4A: 40-50s, [short role], annoying, cynical,
>   comically hungry.
>   Pregnant Woman: 20s, [short role], loud, eager, aggressive.

SKIRMISHES, Catherine Hayes (1982)   Faber and Faber
                        or Harvey Unna & Stephen Durbridge, Ltd.
3w

Two sisters clash during a death vigil for their mother starkly
revealing their jealousies, conflicts, and personal differences.

>   Jean: late 30s, [lead], bitter, resentful, childless, had
>   the responsibility of caring for mother during her
>   illness, tired, exhausted and stressed.
>   Rita: early 30s, [lead], mother of three young children,
>   lives a distance from mother, kind, thoughtful towards
>   mother.
>   Mother: 60-70s, [supporting role], bed ridden, stroke vic-
>   tim, says little but on stage throughout the entire play,
>   left side paralyzed, speaks with great difficulty.

SLAM THE DOOR SOFTLY, Clare Booth Luce, (1970)   Dram. Pl. Ser.
                                        or Best Short Plays 72
1w 1m

Modern day Nora walks out on her husband giving her reasons from
the new consciousness of 1970. Short play.

>   Nora: 30s, [lead], housewife who seeks liberation from do-
>   mestic trap, angry at her repression.

SNOWANGEL, Lewis John Carlino (1963)   Dram. Pl. Ser.
1w 1m

Graphic portrait of a prostitute's pathetic encounter with a
lonely man trying in vain to recreate a scene with a lost love.

>   Connie: 20-30s, [lead], joking, kind, gets drunk, has been
>   around a lot, hard exterior only partially hides vulnera-
>   bility and sensitivity underneath.

SOMETHING UNSPOKEN, Tennessee Williams (1945)   Dram. Pl. Ser.
                                          or 27 Wagonsful of Cotton

2w

An arrogant Southern woman politically maneuvering for an office
in the Confederate Daughters organization is thwarted.
Short play.

>   Miss Cornelia Scott: 60s, [lead], wealthy, grandly preten-
>   tious, aristocratic, haughty.
>   Miss Grace Lancaster: 40s, [supporting role], thin, subser-
>   vient, slightly graying blonde hair. Suggestion of les-
>   bian relationship between the two women.

SPLIT, Michael Weller (1979)   Best Short Plays 79
                                          or Howard Rosenstone & Co.

3w 4m

Sophisticated set of swingers is disrupted because of the break
up of the marriage of two of their members. Short play.

>   Marge: 20-30s, [supporting role], trendy, "far-out" artist
>   friend, concerned for Carol.
>   Carol: 20-30s, [supporting role], breaking up with husband,
>   unhappy.
>   Jean: 20-30s [supporting role], artsy, trendy.

STAGE DIRECTIONS, Israel Horovitz (1977)   Dram. Pl. Ser.
                                          or Best Short Plays 77

2w 1m

Two sisters and a brother in mourning for the recent death of
their parents create an unusual effect telling their tragic story
by reciting stage directions rather than using dialogue. Short
play.

>   Ruth: 30s, [lead], thin, hawk-like, despairing.
>   Ruby: 20s, [lead], small, wren-like, distraught.

STANDARD SAFETY, Julie Bovasso (1976)   Best Short Plays 76
6w 7m

Employees of a large insurance company are engaged in a humorous
struggle to get out from under their oppressive employer. Comedy.

>   Denise: 20-30s, [lead], friendly, affable, but depressed, in
>   analysis.
>   Andrea: 20-30s, [lead], sympathetic, supporting husband
>   through school.
>   Sheila: 20-30s, [supporting role], friend of Denise and
>   Andrea.

Mary Farrell: 30-50s, [short role], petty, punitive secretary to chairman of the board.
Mrs. MacIntosh: 40-60s, [short role], personnel director,
mean, petty, unrealistic expectations.
Louella: 20-30s, [short role], embarrassed, makes a public
confession that she is the secret scribbler.

STEAMING, Nell Dunn, (1981)   Amber Lane Press
6w (1m off-stage voice)

A steam bath is the setting where women come together and share,
without reserve, what is happening in their lives. Sexually
explicit language, nudity.

Violet: 45, [supporting role], proprietor of bath, helpful,
maternal.
Josie: 34, [supporting role], vulgar, kept by lover who
beats her, angry, bored, frustrated.
Mrs. Meadow: 65, [supporting role], prissy, overprotective
of daughter, bossy.
Dawn: 35, [supporting role], daughter of Mrs. Meadow,
humorous food addict, immature, overweight, still not
recovered from emotional trauma.
Nancy: 38, [supporting role], new patron, unsure, nervous,
well off, mother, divorced.
Jane: 38, [supporting role], outgoing, bohemian dress,
student, lonely.

STOOP, Lanford Wilson (1969)   Dram. Pl. Ser.
                                  in volume with The Sand Castle
3w (1 non speaking)

Three elderly women comment with frightening clarity on the
decline in the quality of life. Short play.

first woman: 50s, [lead], heavy set, resigned.
second woman: 60s, [lead], thin, resigned.
third woman: late 50s, [supporting role], non speaking.

STRING, Alice Childress (1971)   Dram. Pl. Ser.
3w 2m

At a neighborhood association picnic in New York City a billfold
containing a large amount of money is lost. Short play. Black
cast.

Mrs. Beverly: 40-50s, [lead], civic minded, hard worker,
conscientious, dresses colorfully.
Mrs. Rogers: 40-50s, [lead], conservative dresser, acts
superior, uppity, bossy.
Maydell: 20s, [lead], pleasant, organizer of picnic.

STUFFINGS, James Prideaux (1973)   Dram. Pl. Ser.
1w 2m

A taxidermist's avid enthusiasm for her work conflicts with her insurance salesman fiancé who is repulsed by taxidermy and wants her to give it up. Short play.

> Gladys Koontz: mid 30s, [lead], plainly dressed, wears
>   glasses, dowdy, fascinated by taxidermy.

SUNSET/SUNRISE, Adele Edling Shank (1979)   West Coast Plays # 4
8w 6m

One night in the lives of a family of brilliant well-educated professionals and their friends in a posh Californian suburb.

> Louise: 47, [lead], wife and mother, compulsive about caring
>   for family, bitter and angry about husband's philan-
>   dering.
> Gem: 48, [lead], successful businesswoman, competent, newly
>   married to fourth husband, a 32 year old teacher.
> Anne: 18, [supporting role], daughter of Louise, bright
>   student, highly allergic to everything, lives in isola-
>   tion, communicates with others via closed circuit TV,
>   well informed, socially undeveloped and shy.
> Diane: 42, [supporting role], neighbor, friend, energetic,
>   compassionate, divorced, career oriented.
> Colleen: 26, [supporting role], secretary, living with
>   Gem's estranged son and mother to his infant son, viva-
>   cious, independent.
> Christine: 20, [short role], daughter of Diane, intelligent,
>   practical, aware.
> Sarah: 19, [short role], friend of Christine.
> Linnea: 25, [short role], beautiful, wealthy, fashionable,
>   dating Diane's ex-husband, self centered, spoiled.

SURPRISE SURPRISE, Michel Tremblay (1975)   Talonbooks
            in volume with La Duchesse de Langais and other Plays
3w

Chaotic mix-up occurs when two women talking on the telephone attempt to plan a surprise party for a friend.

> Jeannine: 20-30s, [lead], well balanced, tries to calm down
>   others, sensible.
> Laurette: 20-30s, [lead], bossy, talks tough.
> Madeline: 20-30s, [lead], believes the others are plotting
>   against her, becomes furious, seeking revenge.

TALKING WITH..., Jane Martin (1982)   Samuel French
11w

A series of monologues reveal in rich detail a broad range of personal viewpoints, experiences and characters.

> Fifteen Minutes: 20-40s, [lead], seasoned performer carries
>   on a conversation with the audience wondering what their
>   lives are like.
> Scraps: 20-30s, [lead], kinky comic housewife who lives in
>   a fantasy world of Oz and vacuums the floor wearing a
>   brightly colored patchwork costume based on a character
>   from her fantasy.
> Clear Glass Marbles: 20-40s, [lead], a woman describes how
>   her mother refused to allow a terminal disease to dampen
>   her spirits.
> Audition: 20-30s, [lead], a nervous, desperate, flaky woman
>   is auditioning for a role in a play.
> Rodeo: 20-40s, [lead], a robust rodeo rider sadly describes
>   the changes that are spoiling the rodeo world.
> Twirler: 20s, [lead], twirling takes on a mystical light and
>   is described as blue collar Zen.
> Lamps: 40s and over, [lead], a woman in later years
>   describes how she used lamps to fill the voids.
> Handler: teens-20s, [lead], a member of a religious cult
>   that handles poisonous snakes as part of their rituals
>   describes her experiences.
> Dragons: 20-30s, [lead], a woman laboring in childbirth.
> French Fries: 20-50s, [lead], satiric piece about a woman
>   whose favorite food is a hamburger from MacDonald's.
> Marks: 20-40s, [lead], a woman with tatoos covering her
>   body describes her philosophy.

TALLEY'S FOLLY, Lanford Wilson (1980)   Dram. Pl. Ser.
1w 1m

Matt woos Sally and convinces her to marry him. Comedy.

> Sally: 30s, [supporting role], thin, attractive, slight
>   Ozark accent, unmarried and embarrassment to her family
>   because she is unable to bear children.

TENNESSEE, Romulus Linney (1980)   Dram. Pl. Ser.
3w 3m

An old woman returns to her former home a log house in Appalachian North Carolina. Short play.

> Old Woman: 70-80s or beyond, [lead], strong willed, eccen-
>   tric.
> Mary: 20s, [supporting role], caring for infant, homespun
>   hill woman.
> Neighbor: 70-80s, [short role], friend of old woman.

THIRD AND OAK, Marsha Norman (1978)   Dram. Pl. Ser.
2w

Two women with very different personalities meet in a laundromat
and unwillingly share personal secrets. Short play.

>   Alberta: 50-60s, [lead], meticulous, quiet, refined, self
>   contained, holding pain of her husband's recent death
>   inside.
>   Deedee: 20s, [lead], loquacious, chatter box, rowdy, common,
>   lively, open, direct.

THIS BIRD OF DAWNING SINGETH ALL NIGHT LONG,   Phillip Hayes Dean
    (1971)   Dram. Pl. Ser.
2w

Hostile encounter between two women shows some typical problems
of black/white relations. Nancy, a black woman, claims to be the
long lost twin sister of Anne, a white woman.

>   Anne   Jillett: mid 30's, [lead], nervous, frightened,
>   bigoted, patronizing.
>   Nancy Ferrett: mid 30's, [lead], heavily stereotyped,
>   wears a bandana, talks with a deep southern accent.

THYMUS VULGARIS, Lanford Wilson (1981)   Dram. Pl. Ser.
2w 1m

A former Las Vegas dancer on the day of her wedding to a wealthy
tycoon goes back home to rescue her mother from an impoverished
life in a rundown trailer park.

>   Evelyn: 35, [lead], garishly dressed, vivid hair color,
>   likable, practical, common, human, down-to-earth.
>   Ruby: 50-60s, [lead], warm, loving, common, depressed, many
>   times married.

TODAY IS INDEPENDENCE DAY, William Hanley (1962)   Dram. Pl. Ser.
1w 1m

Dialogue between a woman who wants to improve herself and her cab
driver husband who is content to leave things the way they are,
at a point where their love life is going stale.

>   Evalyn: late 30s, [lead], attractive, intelligent, sensual,
>   interested in cultural things, analyzing her emotions,
>   wanting more from life.

TOP GIRLS, Caryl Churchill, (1982)   Methuen
7w (doubling)

The newly appointed director of an employment agency dines with
great women from the past, examines how successful women manage
their lives, and deals with the pressures being successful puts
on her personal life.

> Marlene: 30s, [lead], powerful, no nonsense, career minded,
>   ambitious, high achiever.
> Isabella Bird: [supporting role], indomitable, world travel-
>   er, lived in Edinburgh, 1831-1904.
> Lady Nijo: [supporting role], Japanese courtesan, became
>   Buddhist nun and traveled through Japan on foot.
> Dull Gret: [supporting role], from a painting by Brueghel,
>   in apron and armour leads a crowd of women.
> Pope Joan: [supporting role], believed to have been pope in
>   854 till 856.
> Patient Griselda: [supporting role], character from Canter-
>   bury Tales, the obedient wife.
> Joyce: 30s, [supporting role], sister of Marlene, stayed
>   home, cared for family, resentful.
> Win: [supporting role], staff member of agency, affair with
>   married man, ambitious, hard, dynamic, quick.
> Louise: 40s, [short role], client looking for job, con-
>   scientious, hard working.
> Nell: [supporting role], staff of employment agency, tough,
>   ambitious, hard.
> Angie: 16, (played by adult), [supporting role], childish,
>   niece of Marlene, enthusiastic admirer of Marlene.
> Kit: 12, (played by adult), [supporting role], cohort of
>   Angie, troubled, argumentative.
> Mrs. Kidd: 40s-50s, [short role], angry, whining, wife of
>   man who lost out to Marlene for promotion.
> Jeanine: 20, [short role], seeking a better job, not sure of
>   what she wants, moderate skills.
> Shona: 21, [short role], client seeking job, brash, cheeky,
>   fabricates job experience.
> Waitress: [short role], non speaking.

A TOUCH OF MARBLE, Dan Potter (1958)   Best Short Plays 58
4w 2m

Melodrama about a woman who can't let herself love or get close
to others.

> Helen: mid 30s, [lead], hesitant, guarded, fearful, tense,
>   plays young girl in flash back.
> Honey: teens, [short role], beautiful, slim, vain, unhappy.
> Miss Carroll: 30-50s, [short role], brisk school administra-
>   tor.
> Aunt Margaret: 30-50s, [short role], school teacher, exacer-
>   bated nerves, bitter, tries to cheer up young Helen.

TREVOR, John Bowen (1968)   Samuel French
                                                     or Best Short Plays 70

4w 4m

Fast paced mix-up occurs when two lesbian women sharing a flat
have both sets of parents drop in to meet a lover and a fiancé
who don't exist. Comedy. British. Short play.

> Sarah: late 20s, [lead], good paying job, upper-middle
>   class, raised with free thinking philosophy.
> Jane: late 20s, [lead], good paying job, upper-middle class,
>   raised with conventional philosophy.
> Mrs. Lawrence: late 50s, [supporting role], Sarah's mother,
>   free-thinker from the suburbs.
> Mrs. Kempton: late 50s, [supporting role], Jane's mother,
>   conventional middle class matron.

TROUBLE IN MIND, Alice Childress (1955)   Black Theater
3w 6m

A troupe of actors doing a play about racial problems have their
own personal differences erupt during rehearsal. Obie winner.
Black roles.

> Wiletta: 40-50s, [lead], savvy, sophisticated, black player,
>   speaks her mind, good singer.
> Millie: 35, [supporting role], elegantly dressed, black
>   player, wears mink coat, experienced, unhappy, cynical.
> Judy: 20, [supporting role], middle class, white player,
>   first acting job, naive, supportive.

THE TWELVE POUND LOOK, J.M. Barrie (1914)   Samuel French
2w 2m

The smug self-satisfaction of a conventional man about to be
knighted is shaken by the unexpected appearance of his unconventional former wife. Short play.

> Kate: late 30s-40s, [lead], self reliant, unassuming, sure
>   of herself, has her own trade (typist), quick witted,
>   serene, former wife.
> Lady Sims: 30s-40s, [supporting role], dutiful, present
>   wife, dependent on servants, proud, dressed very expen-
>   sively, uncertain about herself.

TWIGS, George Furth (1971)   Samuel French
4w 7m

Four interconnected one-act plays. In the New York production all
four female parts were played by the same performer.

Emily An attractive divorcee is courted by a moving man working in her house.

> Emily: 30s, [lead], stylish, lively, outgoing, intense.

Celia   A housewife is bored by her bigoted husband's sports discussions and beer drinking.

> Celia: 40-50s, [lead] , garish, kind, sensitive, generous, common.

Dorothy A suburban housewife celebrates her 25th wedding anniversary.

> Dorothy: [lead], 40-50s, traditional, ordinary, very maternal, humorous.

Ma   The aging Irish mother of the above three women who decides to finally marry their father.

> Ma: 70s, [lead], failing but tough, sharp, cantankerous, moves with great difficulty.

TWO O'CLOCK FEEDING, Madeline Puccioni (1978) West Coast Plays #4
3w 3m

Compassionate portrayal of a new mother married to a busy resident doctor.   The strains brought on by the baby's arrival lead to child abuse. Adult material.

> Louise: 30, [lead], well-educated, accomplished poet, attractive, overweight, exhausted from lack of sleep, angry because husband is never home, desperate.
> Marie: 40s, [supporting role], friend of Louise, also wife of doctor, experienced mother of four, active, survives pressures by drinking.
> Dr. Simmons: 50s, [short role], [black], staff pediatrician, supportive, professional.

TWO SIDES OF DARKNESS, Edwin Procunier (1959) Best Short Plays 58
5w 4m

The futility of war is addressed by the women who lose their men in both ancient Greek and modern times.

> Melena: teens-early 20s, [supporting role], ancient Greek, shy, in love with shepherd.
> Jenny: teens-early 20s, [supporting role], modern city dweller, in love with car mechanic.
> Chorus of three women: any age, [supporting roles], in the style of classical Greek chorus with some solo recitations.

UNCOMMON WOMEN, Wendy Wasserstein (1978)   Dram. Pl. Ser.
9w

On their six-year reunion graduates of Mount Holyolk College compare notes on their present lives and flashback to scenes from college days.

> Kate Quinn: late 20s, [supporting role], highly respected by classmates, confident, brilliant lawyer.
> Samatha Stewart: late 20s, [supporting role], practical, traditional, married to actor.
> Muffet DiNicola: late 20s, [supporting role], independent, but a romantic with no career direction, insurance seminar hostess.
> Holly Kaplan: late 20s, [supporting role], working on her third M.A., wealthy family, anti-establishment attitudes.
> Rita Altabel: late 20s, [supporting role], reputation for promiscuity in college, very outspoken about sex, was on a DAR scholarship, at reunion she is "getting into her head".
> Leilah: college age, [short role], bright, former room mate of Kate, feels inadequate in comparison with Kate.
> Carter: college age, [short role], new to group, freshman, quiet.
> Susie Friend: early 20s, [supporting role], smug, self righteous, pompous.
> Mrs. Plumm: 70s, [supporting role], prim house mother.

THE UNDERSTANDING, Angela Huth (1982)   Amber Lane Press
                                                  or Curtis Brown, Ltd.
4w 1m

Acton and Leonard have been in love for many years. But he is married to her sister, Eva, so they hold back expression of their love until after her death.

> Eva: 65-75, [lead], Leonard's wife, weary, health failing, preparing to die, terse, genteel, tense.
> Acton: 65-75, [lead], quiet, patient, kind, loving, copper-red hair.
> Kate: 18, [lead], student who comes to work for family, red hair, artistic, enthusiastic, intelligent.
> Lydia: 65-75, [supporting role], sister of Eva and Acton, bossy, conservative, suspicious.

UP THE DOWN STAIRCASE, Bel Kaufman (1969)   Dramatic Pub. Co.
18w 12m

Idealistic new teacher comes to grips with reality of inner-city high school and triumphs over obstacles.

> Sylvia Barrett: early 20s, [lead], new teacher, attractive, enthusiastic, sensitive.

Beatrice Schachter: 30s, [supporting role], experienced
   teacher, attractive, cynical about teaching.
Ellen: 20s, [supporting role], friend who receives letters
   from Sylvia, suburban housewife.
four short parts for school staff members.
eleven short parts for high school students.

VERONICA'S ROOM, Ira Levin (1973)   Samuel French
2w 2m

A college woman falls into a trap when she is persuaded to imper-
sonate a dead woman from a wealthy Boston family.
Mystery-thriller.

Susan: 20s [lead], university student, wholesome, well
   balanced, typical, pretty.
The woman: 40-60s, [lead], changes identities several times
   from elderly Irish domestic with a slight brogue to the
   lady of the manor, mysterious, insane.

A VERY RICH WOMAN, Ruth Gordon (1960)   Samuel French
        adapted from the play by Philippe Heriat
8w 7m

The daughters of a wealthy widow attempt to get their mother
declared incompetent in order to gain control of the family
fortune.

Mrs. Lord: 75, [lead], looks younger than her years, vital,
   chic, snappy dresser, wears make-up, wants to live it up.
Mrs. Minot: 74, [supporting role], looks older than her
   years, friend of Mrs. Lord, proper Bostonian, conservative dresser.
Edith: 40-50s, [supporting role], Mrs. Lord's daughter,
   pretty, chic, smart, mundane, greedy, pretentious, dis-
   honest.
Ursala: 40-50s, [supporting role], Mrs. Lord's daughter,
   pretty, chic, artificial, shallow, self-centered.
Daphne: 17, [supporting role], granddaughter of Mrs. Lord,
   fashionable, trendy, very self assured, sympathetic to
   grandmother.
Mae: 60s, [short role], uniformed maid, white hair.
Miss Moran: age unspecified, [short role], nurse attending
   Mrs. Lord.
Pearl: early 20s, [short role], secretary to Mrs. Lord,
   "looks like a Wellesley senior," sharp.

VICTORY ON MRS. DANDYWINE'S ISLAND, Lanford Wilson (date)
                                              Dram. Pl. Ser.
3w 2m

Parody of the highly mannered style of Oscar Wilde where the very proper structured regime of Mrs. Dandywine is disrupted by the appearance of an unexpected man. Short play.

Mrs. Dandywine: over 50, [lead], stout, perfect manners, meticulous elocution, superior voice.
Miss Companion: over 50, [lead], thin, refined, hair turning gray, impressionable, excitable.
Miss Liveforever: over 50, [short role], red hair, wild makeup, outspoken in the extreme, total lack of manners.

VIVAT! VIVAT! REGINA!, Robert Bolt (1971)   Samuel French
4-5w 27m

Late 16th century England, France, and Scotland is the setting for the story of the two queens, Elizabeth and Mary, the price of being queen and the toll it takes on their personal lives.

Mary, Queen of Scots: age from 17-45, [lead], beautiful, brave, refined, follows her heart, sympathetic, subjective.
Elizabeth I: age range from late 20s to 50s, [lead], brilliant, willful, highly strung, highly disciplined, follows her intellect, hides resentment.
Catherine de Medici: 40-50s, [short role], (role omitted in later versions of script)
1st court lady: [short role]
2nd court lady: [short role]

A VOICE OF MY OWN, Elinor Jones (1979)   Dram. Pl. Ser.
flexible casting

Women's history narrated by a series of famous personalities telling how first women writers used "anonymous" and male pseudonyms before they could speak in their own voices.

VOICES, Susan Griffin (1975)   Samuel French
5w

Five women at different stages of life describe their experiences in monologue form, ie., no interaction between characters.

Rosalinde: 19-20, [supporting role], art student, well adjusted, fanciful imagination, wanted to join circus as child.
Erin: 28, [supporting role], unhappy childhood, painful life, grieving over death of twin brother.
Maya: 35, [supporting role], working on a Ph.D. dissertation, struggling single mother of two children, former student radical.
Grace: 46, [supporting role], feels useless since children have grown up and left.

Kate: late 60s-early 70s, [supporting role], stage and screen performer who choose career over family, courageous, colorful life.

WAITING FOR THE PARADE, John Murrell (1980)   Samuel French
5w

The bravery and heroism of five women in Canada coping with the trials on the home front during World War II.

Eve: 20s, [supporting role], teacher, escapes into fantasies, naive, fresh-scrubbed.
Catherine: early 30s, [supporting role], well-balanced, practical, extremely lonely, misses husband away at war, has affair with another man, mother of small children.
Marta: 30s, [supporting role], persecuted because she is of German descent, timid at first, then angry.
Margaret: 50s, [supporting role], mother worrying about sons, pessimistic, fearful, worries constantly.
Janet: late 30s, [supporting role], strong, bossy, overly conscientious, takes on heavy volunteer load because she feels guilty that her husband was exempted from military.

WEST SIDE WALTZ, Ernest Thompson (1982)   Dram. Pl. Ser.
3w 2m

An elderly woman resists the attempts of her well-meaning but boorish neighbor to move in with her, hires a companion, and sets an example of strength and determination for her friends.

Margaret Mary: 73, [lead], staunch, proud, peppery, sense of humor, emotionally distant, plays piano.
Clara: 56, [lead], rotund, bright make-up, jolly, plays violin, overprotective.
Robin: 30s, [supporting role], pretty, Brooklyn accent, talks in slang, outrageous dress, nutty.

WINE IN THE WILDERNESS, Alice Childress (1969)   Dram. Pl. Ser.
2w 3m

A woman who is modeling for a painter friend is stung when she finds out he considers her ugly. Takes place during burning and looting of urban riots. Short play. Black cast.

Tommy: 30s, [lead], factory worker, uneducated, unsophisticated, wears wig, disoriented because her apartment has been burned, mis-matched clothes, angry.
Cynthia: 20s, [supporting role], social worker, dresses well, educated, tried being reasonable to get ahead in the white people's world, but now disillusioned.

WINGS, Arthur Kopit (1978)   Samuel French
4w 3m

In a dream-like sequence of disorientation a woman goes through the experience of having a stroke, comes back to reality, and fights to regain normalcy.

> Emily Stilson: 70s, [lead], overwhelmed by her experience, frightened, frustrated.
> Amy: 20-30s, [supporting role], therapist, kind, profession-al, group instructor of stroke victims.
> Mrs. Timmins: 60 plus, [short role], stroke victim.
> Nurses: two short roles.

WOMANSPEAK, Gloria Goldsmith (1976)   Pioneer Drama Ser.
12w

Woman's history and problems are described impactfully by eminent figures from the past.   Suggested use of visuals such as slides in background to go along with dialogue. Short play.

> Contemporary Woman: 20-40, [lead], central figure who converses with women from the past.
> Abigail Adams: [supporting role], writer, scholar, advocate of women's rights, lived during American revolution, wife of John Adams.
> Sojourner Truth: [suppporting role], black slave, eloquent spokesperson for civil rights circa 1850.
> Harriet Beecher Stowe: [supporting role], abolitionist, highly influential author of Uncle Tom's Cabin which exposed the evils of slavery.
> Anna Carroll: [supporting role], researcher, author of Tennessee Plan which helped the North to win the Civil war.
> Susan B. Anthony: [supporting role], organizer of women's suffrage campaign.
> Victoria Woodhull: [supporting role], advocate for equal rights, abortion, and free love, ran for U.S. president.
> Mother Jones: [supporting role], courageous organizer of the United Mine Workers.
> Adelita: [supporting role], soldier in New Mexico in 1913, follower of Pancho Villa.
> Margaret Sanger: [supporting role], leader of the birth control movement in 1917.
> Eleanor Roosevelt: [supporting role], advocate for social causes, writer, lecturer, wife of Franklin Roosevelt.
> Emma Goldman: [supporting role], anarchist, activist.

THE WOODS, David Mamet (1979)   Samuel French
1w 1m

The end of summer at a vacation house in a beautiful spot in the woods sets a poetic mood for a love story between a young man and woman. Sexually explicit language.

>   Ruth: 20-30s, [lead], outgoing, convivial, strong willed,
>   outspoken.

A YOUNG LADY OF PROPERTY, Horton Foote (1955)   Dram. Pl. Ser.
6w 3m

Set in a small Texas town in 1925, this story revolves around a
girl of 15 who fantasizes about becoming a movie star and about
the house her dead mother left her; and deals with her indigent
father's new marriage.

>   Wilma Thompson: 15, [lead], spirited, has a certain style
>   about her, good looking,
>   Arabella Cookenboo: 15, [supporting role], Wilma's side
>   kick, shy, insecure, takes Wilma's lead,
>   Miss Gert: 40s, [supporting role], Wilma's aunt, has raised
>   her since death of mother, tall, good looking, solid.
>   Minna: 40s, [supporting role], thin, strong, black woman,
>   domestic working for Gert, maternal.
>   Mrs. Leighton: 35, [short role], engaged to Wilma's father,
>   warm, attractive, gracious.
>   Miss Martha Davenport: 40-plus, [short role], giddy post
>   office clerk.

THE ROLES CLASSIFIED

Age Groupings

The following is an analysis of roles according to the age of the character. This does not mean the age of the performer has to rigidly adhere to the age of the character. Often a play will span over many years in a character's life and the performer must convey the different ages by means of body language and make up. Generally it is more believable if a performer plays characters who range within 10 years older or younger than her real age.

Character Ages 20 and Younger

ABSENT FRIENDS
  Evelyn: [supporting role], stylish and trendy.

AGNES OF GOD
  Agnes: [lead], innocent nun, sheltered, has miraculous powers.

AM I BLUE?
  Ashbe: [lead], unhappy and neglected, but optimistic and able to find beauty and happiness in unexpected corners.
  Clareece: [bit part], teeny bopper.

AUGUSTUS
  Helene: [short role], rides bicycle, gentle, polite.

AUNTIE MAME
    Sally Cato MacDougal: [short role], Southern belle.
    Agnes Gooch: [short role], plain, transforms into sexy
        woman.
    Gloria Upson: [short role], snobbish, narrow minded, bland.
    Pegeen Ryan: [short role], wholesome, kind.

THE AUTOGRAPH HOUND
    Cissie: [supporting role], plain, awkward, ill-fitting
        clothes, lethargic.

THE AUTUMN GARDEN
    Sophie Tuckerman: [supporting role], war refugee, over-
        polite, shy.

THE BATHTUB
    Joyce: [lead], artistic, intelligent, neurotic, infantile.
    Leann: [supporting role], patient, reasonable roommate.

BEAUTY AND THE BEAST
    Beauty: [lead], youngest daughter of merchant, lovely,
        kind, tender-hearted, generous, optimistic, hard worker,
        loves animals.
    Hyacinth: [supporting role], spoiled, self-centered, ill-
        tempered, lazy, greedy, frivolous, second daughter of
        merchant.
    Petunia: [supporting role], spoiled, self-centered, ill-
        tempered, lazy, greedy, eldest daughter.
    Mary Jane: [short role], listener for Mrs. Crunch's story.

BEDROOM FARCE
    Kate: [supporting role], clowns, humorous, bickering,
        joking.
    Jan: [supporting role], trendy.
    Susannah: [supporting role], in emotional crisis, throwing
        tantrums.

BELL, BOOK, AND CANDLE
    Gillian: [lead], graceful, beautiful, has supernatural pow-
        ers.

LES BELLES SOEURS
    Linda: [supporting role], progressive, rebellious, im-
        patient.
    Lise: [supporting role], pregnant, unmarried, ambitious.
    Ginette: [short role], depressed, low self esteem.

BLACK GIRL
    Billie Jean: [lead], hopeful, wanting more from life, angry.
        [black].
    Norma: [supporting role], slightly overweight, young mother.
        [black].
    Ruth Ann: [supporting role], young mother. [black]
    Netta: [short role], going to college to become a teacher.
        [black].

BLANK PAGES
     Carole: [lead], attractive, plumpish, self deprecating,
          charming, witty.

BLIND DATE
     Angie: [lead], lively, robust, impatient with herself.

BLOOD PHOTO
     Elizabeth Goodman: [supporting role], older sister, refined,
          college educated, intelligent, conservative.
     Camile Benedetto: [supporting role], younger sister, common,
          plain, teased hair, fake fur.

BRINGING IT ALL BACK HOME
     Daughter: [supporting role], mindless pom pom girl, chews
          gum, bickers with brother.
     Miss Horne: [supporting role], svelte, TV newscaster, tough,
          outspoken. [black].

BUTTERFLIES ARE FREE
     Jill: [lead], lively, fresh, artsy, reading for part in off
          Broadway production.

CANADIAN GOTHIC
     Jean: [lead], in conflict between creative and practical
          forces within her.

CASTLE IN THE VILLAGE
     Lydia: [lead], warm hearted, glamorous.
     Mrs. Hill: [short role], pregnant apartment seeker.

CHALK GARDEN
     Laurel: [lead], rich, insolent granddaughter, feels unloved.

CHARACTER LINES
     twin sisters played by same actor: [supporting role].
       Evelyn: tells stories of flying saucers.
       Ginger: bright, mature, having an affair with older man.

CHILDREN OF A LESSER GOD
     Sarah: [lead], deaf from birth, closes herself off, hostile.
     Lydia: [supporting role], hearing impaired, soft, timid.
     Edna Klein: [supporting role], awkward with deaf people.

CHOCOLATE CAKE
     Joellen: [lead], slightly overweight, low self image, timid.

CLARA'S OLE MAN
     Big Girl: [lead], heavy, powerful, bully, coarse, domineer-
          ing. [black].
     Clara: [supporting role], slow, feline, submissive. [black].
     Baby Girl: [short role], mentally retarded, wears much make
          up, uses generous amounts of profanity. [black].

A CLEARING IN THE WOODS
    Gina: [lead], conscientious, edgy, having marital problems.
    Nora: [supporting role], idealistic, intellectual, rebel-
        lious.
    Jigee: [supporting role], needing love, angry at being
        neglected.
    Hazelmae: [short role], frivolous, pretentious, overweight.

THE COAL DIAMOND
    Inez: [lead], tall, thin, awkward, chews gum, smokes Camels.
    Betty Jean: [lead], peroxide blonde, pregnant.
    Pearl: [lead], new in town, feels less intelligent than
        others.

THE COCKTAIL PARTY
    Celia: [supporting role], confused, loves Lavinia's husband.
    Lavinia: [supporting role], has just left her husband.

CONFESSIONS OF A FEMALE DISORDER
    Ronnie: [lead], time span from puberty to late 20s, search-
        ing for identity.
    Coop: [lead], in love with Ronnie, free spirit.
    Cheerleaders 1, 2, & 3: [supporting roles], play ensemble in
        several short scenes.
    Liz: [short role], college roommate of Ronnie and Coop.

THE CORRUPTERS
    Carol Ramirez: [lead], convict, drug crimes, prostitution.
    Boots: [supporting role], tough boss of inmates, domineer-
        ing.
    Mary: [supporting role], inmate, befriends Carol, fearful.
    Frankie: [supporting role], inmate, rough cohort of Boots.
    Liz: [short role], inmate, scared of Boots.
    Marie Caliante: [short role], prostitute up before the
        judge.

A COUPLA WHITE CHICKS SITTING AROUND TALKING
    Maude Mix: [lead], typical New York suburban housewife.
    Hannah Mae Bindler: [lead], newly arrived wife from Texas.

CRIMES OF THE HEART
    Lenny: [lead], plump, shy with men, self-conscious, lonely.
    Meg: [lead], unstable, wild, nightclub singer, bad reputa-
        tion.
    Babe: [lead], shot husband, frightened, unsophisticated,
        likable.
    Chick: [supporting role], status conscious, judgmental,
        prudish.

THE CURIOUS SAVAGE
    Wilhelmina: [supporting role], attractive, efficient, staff
        of sanitarium.
    Fairy May: [supporting role], beauty hid by severe dress.
    Florence: [supporting role], sweet, graceful, eager to
        please.

THE DANCERS
   Emily: [supporting role], popular, well dressed.
   Mary Catherine: [supporting role], loyal, believes she is
      plain.
   Waitress: [short role], works in drugstore.
   Velma: [short role], friend of Mary Catherine.

THE DARK OF THE MOON AND THE FULL
   Patsy: [supporting role], granddaughter, slim, graceful,
      pretty.

DESIGN FOR LIVING
   Helen Carver: [short role], conservative, wealthy, well
      dressed.

THE DRAPES COME
   Barbara: [lead], high school senior, harsh, cruel, disorder-
      ly, then changes to timid and withdrawn.

DUSA, FISH, STAS, AND VI
   Violet: [lead], waif, punkish, physically weak, sometimes
      on uppers.
   Dusa: [lead], artistic, husband has run off with their two
      children.
   Fish: [lead], from upper middle class background, intelli-
      gent, active in political causes, lover has left her for
      another.
   Stas: [lead], big attractive, physio therapist, loves
      science, very intelligent, raising money for college
      education by being a call girl at night.

EDUCATING RITA
   Rita: [lead], changes from common and uneducated to ultra
      sophisticate.

THE EFFECT OF GAMMA RAYS
   Ruth: [lead], older daughter, high strung, pretty, shallow.
   Tillie: [lead], younger daughter, shy, plain, highly intel-
      ligent.
   Janice: [short role], pompous winner of science prize.

FAVOURITE NIGHTS
   Catherine: [lead], striking looking, honest, direct, English
      instructor, knowledgeable, intellectually gifted, cool,
      self-contained.
   Sarah: [supporting role], Catherine's younger sister,
      anxiously awaiting the results of her exams, not as
      bright as her sister, naive, worried.
   The girl: [short role], casino employee.

FEFU AND HER FRIENDS
   Fefu: [lead], crazy in an absurd way, plays with guns,
      has strange marriage.

Cindy: [supporting role], close friend of Fefu, loyal, tolerant, good singing voice.
Christine: [supporting role], timid, conformist, childish, reads French.
Julia: [supporting role], traumatized by a hunting accident, paralyzed in wheelchair, having hallucinations.
Emma: [supporting role], concerned about sex, outgoing.
Paula: [supporting role], discouraged about her love relationship, sings Schubert's Who is Sylvia?
Cecilia: [supporting role], intelligent, self-assured.
Sue: [supporting role], humorous, clown.

FINISHING TOUCHES
Felicia: [supporting role], beautiful actor.
Elsie: [supporting role], student, not very bright, big hearted.

FIRST BREEZE OF SUMMER
Lucretia: [supporting role], beautiful, servant, [black].
Hope: [short role], girl friend of grandson, [black].

THE FLOUNDER COMPLEX
Girl: [supporting role], sweet, easy going, kind, pretty, modest.

FOR COLORED GIRLS
dancers [black].

FORTY CARATS
Trina Stanley: [supporting role], hip pool hustler.

THE FROGS
Maisie: [lead], slim, pretty, bright, efficient, tender hearted.

FUNNYHOUSE OF A NEGRO
Sarah: [lead], insane, hallucinating, angry, long monologues, [black].

GETTING OUT
Arlene: [lead], subdued, just released from jail.
Arlie: [supporting role], Arlene at a younger age, spirited and violent.

GIFT OF MURDER!
Mary: [supporting role], pretty, wholesome, niece.

THE GINGERBREAD LADY
Polly: [supporting role], Evy's daughter, down-to-earth, pretty.

GOD SAYS THERE IS NO PETER OTT
Mary: [lead], pretty, sullen, spoiled, expensively dressed.

GOING TO SEE THE ELEPHANT
    Sara Wheeler: [lead], wholesome, earthy, sincere, kind, long
        hair, good singing voice (sings several songs).
    Etta Bailey; [lead], grew up on prairies, child like,
        unaffected, strange, stoic, traumatized.

GOLDA
    Small girl: [short role], Golda as a young child, also plays
        Sarile as a child, and DP.
    Sister: teen, [short role], also plays young girl, Clara
        teen aged, American girl, DP.

GOODBYE MY FANCY
    Ginny Merrill: [supporting role], serious minded student.
    Mary Nell: [supporting role], Ginny's roommate, superficial.

HAY FEVER
    Sorel Bliss: [lead], concerned for propriety, attractive.
    Jackie Coryton: [supporting role], plain, ingenuous, simple.

THE HORSE LATITUDES
    Mary: [supporting role], daughter, bookworm, sensitive.

HOT L BALTIMORE
    Jackie: [supporting role], violent, fighter, thief, dreamer.
    Girl: [supporting role], sensitive, pretty, prostitute.

I AM A CAMERA
    Sally: [lead], sexually amoral, self-centered, full of life.
    Natalia: [short role], intensely serious, searching for
        truth.

I JUST WANTED SOMEONE TO KNOW
    many short roles portraying women laborers from the past.

I OUGHT TO BE IN PICTURES
    Libby: [lead], angry daughter of divorced parents.

IMPROMPTU
    Lora: [supporting role], innocent, naive, accommodating.

IN THE DESSERT OF MY SOUL
    Josie: [supporting role], had tough life without love.

THE INDEPENDENT FEMALE
    Sarah Bullit: [lead], outspoken feminist, dedicated, quick
        witted, angry.
    Gloria Pennybank: [lead], impressionable, childish, naive,
        preparing to be married, confused.
    Barker: [short role], makes introductory speech at beginning
        of action and sums up at the end of play.

JOE EGG
    Jo: [short role], retarded child, unable to speak, walk, or
        use arms.

JOSEPHINE; THE MOUSE SINGER
    Josephine: [lead], loves to sing.
    Sycophant One: [short role], admirer of Josephine.
    Mouse A, B, C, D, & E.: [short roles], townsfolk.
    Mouse Ghosts: [short roles].

KILLINGS ON THE LAST LINE
    Starkey: [supporting role], ambitious, studying to improve
        job.

THE KNIGHT AT THE TWELFTH SAUCER
    Shanakind: [supporting role], large, unkempt, spoiled,
        gluttonous.

LADIES AT THE ALAMO
    Suits: [supporting role], jolly, fat, undercurrent of power.

LADYHOUSE BLUES
    Helen: [supporting role], pretty, blonde, ravaged by
        tuberculosis.
    Dot: [supporting role], chic, married to wealthy man,
        pregnant.
    Terry: [supporting role], exuberant, "her own woman".
    Eylie: [supporting role], waitress, audacious, sexy.

THE LARK
    Joan: [lead], small, fanatical, brave, defiant, unbending.
    Little Queen: [short role], inept, frivolous, sheltered.
    Agnes Sorel: [short role], fashionable, frivolous.

THE LAST OF MRS LINCOLN
    Mary Harlan: [supporting role], kind, gentle, from wealthy
        family.

THE LAST OF THE RED HOT LOVERS
    Bobbi: [supporting role], nutty actress, nervous, pot
        smoking.

A LATE SNOW
    Quincy: [lead], open, honest, writer, impatient.

LET ME HEAR YOU WHISPER
    Danielle: [supporting role], talky, easy-going, irrespon-
        sible.

LETTERS HOME
    Sylvia: [lead], sensitive artist, writer, mother.

LOOK: WE'VE COME THROUGH
    Belle Dort: [lead], plain, intelligent, book worm, idealis-
        tic.
    Jennifer: [supporting role], vain, trying to be sophis-
        ticated.

LOOSE ENDS
    Susan: [lead], rising professional photographer, talented.

LOVERS
    Mag: [lead], vivacious, full of life.

LOVERS AND OTHER STRANGERS
    Brenda: [lead], mod, attractive, glib defensive facade.
    Wilma: [lead], strong, attractive, sexually assertive.
    Joan: [lead], romantic, limited intelligence.
    Susan: [supporting role], passive, sweet.

THE LOVES OF CASS MCGUIRE
    Tessa: [short role], maid.

LUANN HAMPTON
    LuAnn: [lead], first act: wholesome high school cheerleader,
        second act: 10 years later, hardened beauty operator;
        third act: another 10 years later, matronly beautiful.
    Charmaine: [supporting role], sassy, argumentative, jeering.

LUDLOW FAIR
    Rachel: [lead], dramatic, fast living, glamorous.
    Agnes: [lead], shy, plain, joking and kooky.

LUNCH HOUR
    Carrie: [lead], slender, pretty, kookie, disorganized,
        clumsy.

LUNCH OR SOMETHING
    Pam: [lead], sophisticated, educated, well dressed.
    Janet: [lead], sophisticated, educated, well dressed.

THE MADWOMAN OF CHAILLOT
    Irma: [short role], angelic, kind, waitress.
    Flower girl: [short role], sells flowers.

THE MAIDS
    Madam: [supporting role], wealthy, dramatically gloomy.

MAJOR BARBARA
    Barbara Undershaft: [lead], intelligent, committed, ener-
        getic.
    Jenny Hill: [supporting role], pale, pretty, overwrought,
        pious.
    Sarah Undershaft: [short role], fashionable, slim, mundane.

A MATTER OF GRAVITY
    DuBois: [supporting role], servant, inner conflict, gloomy.
    Shatov: [supporting role], leftist political activist.
    Elizabeth: [supporting role], softer, respects wealth, out-
        spoken.

A MEMBER OF THE WEDDING
    Frankie: [lead], awkward, gangling, boyish, feels inade-
        quate.
    Janice: [short role], pretty but ordinary.
    Doris: [bit part], pretty, popular.
    Helen: [bit part], pretty, popular, happy, well adjusted.

THE MIDNIGHT CALLER
    Helen: [lead], strong, sensible, warm.
    Alma Jean: [lead], haughty, prim, hard to please.
    Cutie: [supporting role], tolerant, hard working, sensitive.

MIMOSA PUDICA
    Dianne: [lead], friendly, vivacious, plain yet attractive.

THE MIRACLE WORKER
    Annie Sullivan: [lead], visually impaired, strong-willed,
        tough.
    Helen: [lead], wild, undisciplined, blind and deaf, unre-
        strained, extreme frustration.
    Kate Keller: [supporting role], sweet, tender hearted,
        loving.
    Martha: [short role], black child.

A MOON FOR THE MISBEGOTTEN
    Josie: [lead], powerful, large and strong, but still femi-
        nine, Irish.

MY COUSIN RACHEL
    Louise: [supporting role], innocent, rich, pretty, idealis-
        tic.

MY CUP RANNETH OVER
    Paula: [lead], attractive, trim, unpublished writer, smug.
    Yucca: [lead], easy going, scrawny, singer, tousled hair.

MY SISTER IN THIS HOUSE
    Christine: [lead], servant, assured, neat, quick, talented,
        oppressed.
    Lea: [lead], servant, younger sister, insecure, clumsy,
        sheltered.
    Isabelle Danzard: [supporting role], daughter of mistress,
        inept, domineered over by mother.

NORMAN CONQUESTS
    Annie: [supporting role], careless about grooming and
        sloppy.

OH DAD, POOR DAD
    Rosalie: [supporting role], robust, lively, lusty, se-
        ductive.

ONCE A CATHOLIC
    Mary Mooney: [lead], plain, freckled, good singing voice.
    Mary McGinty: [supporting role], pretty, blonde, frivolous.

Mary Gallagher: [supporting role], attractive, sensible,
     dark.
Mary O'Grady: [short role], pretty.
Mary O'Hennessy: [short role], fat.
Mary Flanagan: [short role], brainy.
Mary Murphy: [short role], small.

EVERYBODY LOVES OPAL
     Gloria: [supporting role], brash, hard, mean.

OPAL IS A DIAMOND
     Mary: [supporting role], pretty, self-assured campaign
          worker.

OPAL'S BABY
     Verna: [supporting role], shabby, forlorn, dirty, deceptive.

OUT OF OUR FATHER'S HOUSE
     Eliza southgate: [supporting role], frivolous schoolgirl.

A PALM TREE IN A ROSE GARDEN
     Lila: [supporting role], Rose's daughter, quiet, plain,
          smart.
     Barbara: [supporting role], ambitious, wants to become film
          star, insecure.

A PHOENIX TOO FREQUENT
     Dynamene: [lead], beautiful, newly widowed, sorrowful, live-
          ly, healthy.
     Doto: [lead], servant, practical, earthy, comic.

PIZZA
     Grace: [lead], intelligent, creative, not pretty.
     Perla: [short role], new neighbor, exotic dancer, flam-
          boyant, Hispanic.
     Bonsey: [short role], 50s style pin ball playing punk.
     Pizza lady: [short role], delivers pizza.

PLEASE, NO FLOWERS
     Sandy: [short role], attractive, kind, loving niece of Lena.

THE PRIMARY ENGLISH CLASS
     Debbie Westba: [lead], teacher, bright, competent.
     Translator: [supporting role], communicates what others say.
     Yoko Kuzukago: [short role], Japanese speaking, beautiful.

THE PRIME OF MISS JEAN BRODIE
     Sandy: [lead], schoolgirl, bright, misunderstood.
     Jenny: [supporting role], schoolgirl, pretty.
     Mary McGregor: [supporting role], schoolgirl, timid, orphan.

A RAISIN IN THE SUN
     Beneatha: [lead], medical student, confident, lean, intel-
          lectual. [black].

THE RATTLE OF A SIMPLE MAN
    Cyrenne: [lead], outspoken, poised, beautiful, kind,
        haughty.

THE RIMERS OF ELDRITCH
    Eva Jackson: [supporting role], crippled, wistful, dreamy.
    Patsy Johnson: [supporting role], stuck-up, flighty.
    Lena Truit: [short role], friend of Patsy, sensible.

THE RIVER
    The girl: [supporting role], lonely, insecure, unhappy.

THE ROADS TO HOME
    Annie: [lead], delicate, dellusional, often out of touch
        with reality, unable to cope, many tragic experiences,
        good singing voice.

ROOMFUL OF ROSES
    Bridget: [lead], thin, vital, hurt, hides her feelings.
    Jane: [supporting role], bright, realistic.

ROUGE ATOMIQUE
    Wife: [lead], angry, possessive, fearful of losing husband.
    Woman: [lead], loving, attractive, believes man loves her.

SAFE HOUSE
    Hillary: [lead], stylish dress, mod hat, militant radical.
    Ruth: [supporting role], pretty, wants conventional life.
    Tink: [supporting role], skinny, granny glasses, weird.

THE SAND CASTLE
    Joan: [supporting role], daughter, playful college student.
    Sasha: [supporting role], Joan's friend, sexy, outgoing.

THE SECRET AFFAIRS OF MILDRED WILD
    Miss Manley: [supporting role], TV publicity crew, slick,
        tough.
    Evelyn: [short role], TV hostess, announces prizes.

SEPARATE CEREMONIES
    Lauren: [supporting role], daughter, college student.

SHOUT ACROSS THE RIVER
    Christine: [lead], very quiet, sudden outbursts of violence.

SISTER MARY IGNATIUS EXPLAINS IT ALL FOR YOU
    Diane Symonds: [supporting role], singer, miserable, angry.
    Philomena Rostovitch: [short role], unwed mother.

SNOWANGEL
    Connie: [lead], hard, joking, drinks, vulnerability under-
        neath.

SPLIT
    Marge: [supporting role], trendy, "far-out" artist.
    Carol: [supporting role], breaking up with husband, unhappy.
    Jean: [supporting role], artsy, trendy.

STAGE DIRECTIONS
    Ruby: [lead], small, wren-like, distraught.

STANDARD SAFETY
    Denise: [lead], depressed, in analysis.
    Andrea: [lead], supporting husband through school.
    Sheila: [supporting role], friend of Denise and Andrea.
    Mary Farrell: [short role], petty, punitive executive secre-
        tary.
    Louella: [short role], ashamed secret scribbler.

STRING
    Maydell: [lead], pleasant organizer of picnic.

SUNSET/SUNRISE
    Anne: [supporting role], bright student, isolated, shy.
    Colleen: [supporting role], secretary, vivacious, inde-
        pendent.
    Christine: [short role], intelligent, practical, aware.
    Sarah: [short role], friend of Christine.
    Linnea: [short role], beautiful, wealthy, self-centered.

SURPRISE, SURPRISE
    Jeannine: [lead], well-balanced, sensible.
    Laurette: [lead], bossy, talks tough.
    Madeline: [lead], feels persecuted, furious, seeking
        revenge.

TALKING WITH...
    Fifteen Minutes: [lead], seasoned performer carries
        on a conversation with the audience wondering what their
        lives are like.
    Scraps: [lead], kinky comic housewife who lives in
        a fantasy world of Oz and vacuums the floor wearing a
        brightly colored patchwork costume based on a character
        from her fantasy.
    Clear Glass Marbles: [lead], a woman describes how her
        mother refused to allow a terminal disease to dampen
        her spirits.
    Audition: [lead], a nervous, desperate, flaky woman is
        auditioning for a role in a play.
    Rodeo: [lead], a robust rodeo rider sadly describes the
        changes that are spoiling the rodeo world.
    Twirler: [lead], twirling takes on a mystical light and is
        described as blue collar Zen.
    Handler: [lead], a member of a religious cult that handles
        poisonous snakes as part of their rituals describes her
        experiences.
    Dragons: [lead], a woman laboring in childbirth.

French Fries: [lead], satiric piece about a woman whose
favorite food is a hamburger from MacDonald's.

Marks: [lead], a woman with tatoos covering her body
describes her philosophy.

TENNESSEE

Mary: [supporting role], caring for infant, homespun hill
woman.

THIRD AND OAK

Deedee: [lead], loquacious chatter box, rowdy, common,
lively.

TOP GIRLS

Pope Joan: [supporting role], believed to have been pope in
854 till 856.

Patient Griselda: [supporting role], character from Canter-
bury Tales, the obedient wife.

Win: [supporting role], staff member of agency, affair with
married man, ambitious, hard, dynamic, quick.

Nell: [supporting role], staff of employment agency, tough,
ambitious, hard.

Angie: 16, (played by adult), [supporting role], childish,
niece of Marlene, enthusiastic admiration for Marlene.

Kit: 12, (played by adult), [supporting role], cohort of
Angie, troubled, argumentative.

Jeanine: [short role], seeking a better job, not sure of
what she wants, moderate skills.

Shona: [short role], client seeking job, brash, cheeky,
fabricates job experience.

Waitress: [short role], non speaking.

A TOUCH OF MARBLE

Honey: [short role], beautiful, slim, vain, unhappy.

TREVOR

Sarah: [lead], good paying job, free thinker.

Jane: [lead], good paying job, conventional background.

TROUBLE IN MIND

Judy: [supporting role], on first acting job, naive, supportive.

TWO SIDES OF DARKNESS

Melena: [supporting role], ancient Greek, shy, loves
shepherd.

Jenny: [supporting role], modern urbanite, loves car
mechanic.

UNCOMMON WOMEN

Kate Quinn: [supporting role], respected, confident,
brilliant.

Samatha Stewart: [supporting role], practical, traditional.

Muffet DiNicola: [supporting role], independent, no career.

Holly Kaplan: [supporting role], working on her third M.A.

Rita Altabel: [supporting role], outspoken about sex, into
    growth movement.
Leilah: [short role], bright, feels inadequate.
Carter: [short role], new to group, freshman, quiet.
Susie Friend: [supporting role], smug, self-righteous,
    pompous.

THE UNDERSTANDING
    Kate: [lead], student who comes to work for wealthy
        family, red hair, artistic, enthusiastic, intelligent.

UP THE DOWN STAIRCASE
    Sylvia Barrett: [lead], new teacher, attractive, enthusias-
        tic, idealistic.
    Beatrice Schachter: [supporting role], experienced, cynical.
    Ellen: [supporting role], suburban housewife.

VERONICA'S ROOM
    Susan: [lead], student, wholesome, typical, pretty.

A VERY RICH WOMAN
    Daphne: [supporting role], fashionable, trendy, self-
        assured.
    Miss Moran: [short role], nurse attending Mrs. Lord.
    Pearl: [short role], "looks like a Wellesley senior",
        sharp.

VIVAT ! REGINA!
    Mary, Queen of Scots: [lead], beautiful, brave, emotional.
    Queen Elizabeth I: [lead], brilliant, highly disciplined,
        intellectual.
    First Court Lady: [short role].
    Second Court Lady: [short role].

A VOICE OF MY OWN
    flexible casting- one performer can play several roles
        covering famous personalities from women's history.

VOICES
    Rosalinde: [supporting role], art student, fanciful imagina-
        tion.
    Erin: [supporting role], painful life, grieving.

WINE IN THE WILDERNESS
    Cynthia: [supporting role], social worker, well dressed.
        [black].

WINGS
    Amy: [supporting role], therapist, kind, professional.

WOMANSPEAK
    Contemporary Woman: [lead], converses with women from the
        past.
    Mother Jones: [supporting role], courageous organizer of the
        United Mine Workers.

Adelita: [supporting role], soldier in New Mexico in 1913, follower of Pancho Villa.
Emma Goldman: [supporting role], anarchist, activist.

THE WOODS
Ruth: [lead], outgoing, convivial, strong willed, outspoken.

A YOUNG LADY OF PROPERTY
Wilma Thompson: [lead], spirited, special air about her.
Arabella Cookenboo: [supporting role], shy, insecure.

Character Ages 30 to 40

ABSENT FRIENDS
Diana: [lead], tense, suspicious, worrisome.
Evelyn: [supporting role], stylish and trendy.
Marge: [supporting role], enjoys fussing over sick husband.

ABSURD PERSON SINGULAR
Jane: [supporting role], compulsively neat homemaker.
Eve: [supporting role], several comic suicide attempts.

AGNES OF GOD
Mother Miriam Ruth: [lead], mystical nun, defends the church.

AM I BLUE?
Hilda: [short role], outspoken, curt waitress.

AND IF THAT MOCKINGBIRD DON'T SING
Casey: [lead], tired, resolute, undaunted, warm, generous.

AND MISS REARDON DRINKS A LITTLE
Mrs. Pentrano: [short role], comic, sells cosmetics, malaprop.

AUNTIE MAME
Auntie Mame: [lead], courageous, adventuresome, spirited.
Vera: [supporting role], comic, actor, heavy drinker.
Norah Muldoon: [short role], spunky nanny.
Sally Cato MacDougal: [short role], Southern belle.
Agnes Gooch: [short role], comic, transforms into sexy woman.

BEDROOM FARCE
Kate: [supporting role], clowns with husband, humorous bickering.
Jan: [supporting role], trendy, old romance with husband of friend.
Susannah: [supporting role], emotional crisis, frightened.

LES BELLES SOEURS
    Germaine: [lead], gloating, coarse, vulgar, abrasive.
    Pierrette: [supporting role], kindly, caring, feels washed up.

    Lisette: [supporting role], puts on airs, has been to Europe.
    Marie-Ange: [supporting role], overworked housewife, jealous.
    Des-Neiges: [supporting role], desperately lonely.

BITS AND PIECES
    Iris: [lead], intelligent, distraught, committed to her
        quest.
    Helen: [supporting role], supportive sister-in-law.

BONJOUR LA BONJOUR
    Denise: [supporting role], overweight, compulsive over
        eater.
    Monique: [supporting role], paranoid, hypochondriac, always
        taking pills.
    Nicole: [supporting role], kind, gentle, loving.

THE BRIDAL NIGHT
    Miss Regan: [lead], good looking school teacher, independent
        means, solitary.

BRONTOSAURUS
    Assistant: [short role], quiet.

CALM DOWN MOTHER
    any of characters.

CANADIAN GOTHIC
    Jean: [lead], in conflict between creative and limiting
        forces.
    Mother: [short role], loving, sensitive, independent, art-
        istic.

CASTLE IN THE VILLAGE
    Mrs. Hill: [short role], pregnant apartment seeker.

CATSPLAY
    Ilona: [short role], daughter, ambitious professional woman.

THE CHALK GARDEN
    Madrigal: [lead], intense, neat, contained, calm, humorless.
    Olivia: [supporting role], been abroad, wants her daughter
        back.
    Second applicant: [short role], small, energetic, nervous.

CHAPTER TWO
    Jennie Malone: [lead], wise, well-balanced, and chic.
    Faye Medwick: [supporting role], practical, witty, actor.

CHARACTER LINES
    Linda: [lead], successful novelist, under pressure.

CHILDREN OF A LESSER GOD
  Edna Klein: [supporting role], lawyer, naive, awkward.

THE CHINESE RESTAURANT SYNDROME
  Susan Lemmerer: [lead], chic, sophisticated, joking.
  Maggie Stewart: [lead], chic, sophisticated, glib, humorous.

A CLEARING IN THE WOODS
  Virgina: [lead], intelligent, important job, overworked,
    hurting.

THE COAL DIAMOND
  Inez: [lead], tall, thin, chews gum, smokes Camels.
  Pearl: [lead], new in town, feels inadequate.

THE COCKTAIL PARTY
  Celia: [supporting role], confused, searching.
  Lavinia: [supporting role], has just left her husband.

CONFESSIONS OF A FEMALE DISORDER
  Evelyn: [short role], depressed housewife, next door neigh-
    bor.

THE CORRUPTERS
  Rachel Crane: [supporting role], reporter, intelligent.
  Boots: [supporting role], tough boss of inmates, domineer-
    ing.
  Mary: [supporting role], inmate, befriends Carol, fearful.
  Frankie: [supporting role], inmate, rough cohort of Boots.
  Liz: [short role], inmate, scared of Boots.

A COUPLA WHITE CHICKS
  Maude Mix: [lead], typical New York suburban housewife,
    comic.
  Hannah Mae Bindler: [lead], newly arrived wife from Texas,
    comic.

CRIMES OF THE HEART
  Lenny: [lead], plump, shy, self conscious, lonely.

CROWN MATRIMONIAL
  Mary, Princess Royal: [supporting role]
  Duchess of Glouster (Alice): [short role], attractive, very
    shy.
  Duchess of York [short role], pretty, slightly plump.

THE DANCERS
  Inez: [supporting role], overprotective, worried.

A DELICATE BALANCE
  Julia: [supporting role], spoiled, irritable, agitated.

DENTIST AND PATIENT
    Anybody: [lead], naive dentist, honest, gullible chump.
    Anybody else: [lead], the patient, crafty, unscrupulous,
        stingy.

DESIGN FOR LIVING
    Gilda: [lead], fun loving, gay, smart, sophisticated.
    Grace Torrence: [short role], sophisticated.

EVERYBODY HAS TO BE SOMEBODY
    Frances: [supporting role], pretty, was child star, shy,
        private, modest.

THE EYE OF THE BEHOLDER
    Jane: [lead], slim, fair, intellectual, artistic style cool
        and classical.
    Bella: [lead], heavy set, dark, emotional, artistic style
        intense, free, loose, abandoned.
    Leona: [supporting role], model, attractive, opinionated,
        joins in conversation.

FALLEN ANGELS
    Jane: [lead], sophisticated, upper class.
    Julia: [lead], sophisticated, upper class.

FATHER'S DAY
    Louise: [lead], lean, good-looking, cynical and bitter.
    Estelle: [lead], fragile, soft.
    Marian: [lead], tall, dark, articulate.

FIRST BREEZE OF SUMMER
    Gloria: [short role], angry, believes she has been cheated.
        [black].

FOR COLORED GIRLS
    dancers: [supporting roles], [black].

FOR THE USE OF THE HALL
    Terry: [supporting role], long red hair, plump, progressive
        nun.
    Alice: [supporting role], blond, bosomy, cheerful,
        practical.

THE FROGS
    Miss Philips: [lead], sturdy, teacher in local school, sen-
        sitive, aware.

FUNNYHOUSE OF A NEGRO
    Sarah: [lead], insane, hallucinating, angry, [black].
    Landlady: [supporting role], tall, thin.

GETTING OUT
    Ruby: [supporting role], friend and ex-con, tries to help.

GOING TO SEE THE ELEPHANT
    Helene Nichols: [lead], raised in New York, refined,
        Victorian, graceful, under hardships.

A GOOD TIME
    Mandy Morgan: [lead], chic, ballet dancer, cynical, dis-
        illusioned.

THE GREAT NEBULA IN ORION
    Carrie: [lead], well dressed, plumpish, suburban wife and
        mother.
    Louise: [lead], successful dress designer, fashionable,
        smart.

HAY FEVER
    Myra Arundel: [supporting role], ultra-chic, fashionable.
    Jackie Coryton: [supporting role], plain, ingenuous, simple.

THE HORSE LATITUDES
    Neva Jo: [lead], lives in fantasy.

HOT L BALTIMORE
    April: [supporting role], brassy prostitute.
    Suzy: [supporting role], prostitute, "Jewish Marilyn
        Monroe".

HOW THE OTHER HALF LOVES
    Theresa Phillips: [supporting role], feels inadequate,
        frustrated.
    Fiona Foster: [supporting role], well-off, smart,
        sophisticated.
    Mary Detweiler: [supporting role], insecure, timid, bites
        nails.

I JUST WANTED SOMEONE TO KNOW
    several short roles for characters from labor history

I LOST A PAIR OF GLOVES YESTERDAY
    An Actress: [lead], despairing, discouraged, flashes of
        vivaciousness.

IMPROMPTU
    Winifred: [lead], seasoned performer, cynical, brittle.

JACOB'S LADDER
    Leona: [lead], avant guard painter, torn, hurt, single
        parent.

JESSIE AND THE BANDIT QUEEN
    Belle Starr: [lead], strong, forceful, tough but vulnerable.

JOE EGG
    Sheila: [lead], mother of retarded child, jokes to survive.
    Pam: [supporting role], blasé, fashionable, intolerant.

THE KILLING OF SISTER GEORGE
  Alice: [lead], young looking, waits on June hand and foot.
  Mrs. Mercy Croft: [supporting role], business-like assistant
    at BBC.

KILLINGS ON THE LAST LINE
  Hidelman: [supporting role], angry, outspoken, strong,
    muscular. [black].
  Ellis: [supporting role], sneaks baby to work, lacks child
    care. [black].
  Mavis: [supporting role], union rep, company sympathizer.
    [black].

LADIES AT THE ALAMO
  Suits: [supporting role], jolly, fat, undercurrent of power.
  Shirley Fuller: [supporting role], award nominee, energetic,
    active.

THE LADY FROM DUBUQUE
  Jo: [lead], sick and dying from cancer, realistic, angry.
  Lucinda: [supporting role], shallow, caustic.
  Carol: [supporting role], glamorous, not very bright.

THE LARK
  Joan's mother: [short role], loving, supportive.

THE LAST OF RED HOT LOVERS
  Elaine: [supporting role], direct, sexy, craves cigarettes.
  Jeanette: [supporting role], gloomy, despairing, depressed,
    on pills.

A LATE SNOW
  Ellie: [lead], career oriented, wants to avoid criticism.
  Pat: [lead], attractive, witty, holds no punches, self
    assured.

LATER
  Kate: [lead], bossy, stubborn, argumentative, unpredictable.
  Laurie: [lead], married, mother of two adolescent boys,
    softer.

LET ME HEAR YOU WHISPER
  Dr. Crocus: [short role], mean, experiments on animals.
  Ms. Fridge: [short role], assistant, not very bright,
    obedient.
  Danielle: [supporting role], talky janitor, easy-going,
    irresponsible.

LETTERS HOME
  Sylvia: [lead], sensitive artist, writer, poet.

LOOSE ENDS
  Susan: [lead], rising professional photographer, talented.
  Janice: [supporting role], friend of Susan.

Maraya: [supporting role], maternal, earthy, domestic, pregnant.

Selina: [supporting role], Chinese-American, film maker, steady.

A LOVELY SUNDAY FOR CREVE COEUR

Dorothea: [lead], romantic dreamer, fading Southern belle.

Bodey: [lead], German, hard-of-hearing, short, plump, simple.

Helena: [lead], stylish, elegant, arrogant, snobbish.

LOVERS AND OTHER STRANGERS

Wilma: [lead], attractive, sexually assertive, searching.

Cathy: [lead], soft touch, silly, comic.

LUANN HAMPTON

LuAnn: [lead], high school cheerleader, then hardened beauty operator, spans over 30 years of her life.

LUDLOW FAIR

Rachel: [lead], dramatic, fast-living, glamorous.

Agnes: [lead], shy, plain, joking and kooky.

LUNCH HOUR

Nora: [lead], attractive, impeccably dressed, clever, organized.

THE MAIDS

Solange: [lead], angry, bitter, jealous of employer.

Claire: [lead], vengeful, hateful and frustrated.

MAUD GONNE SAYS NO TO THE POET

Izzie: [supporting role], Maud's daughter, practical, serious, sober.

A MEMBER OF THE WEDDING

Mrs. West: [short role], vivacious, blonde hair, dowdy.

THE MIDNIGHT CALLER

Alma Jean: [lead], haughty, prim, hard to please, complaining.

THE MIRACLE WORKER

Kate Keller: [supporting role], sweet, tender hearted, loving, gentle,

Aunt Ev: [short role], loving, supportive, proper, prideful.

Viney: [short role], servant, [black].

MISS MARGARIDA'S WAY

Miss Margarida: [lead], prototype of totalitarian dictator.

MOJO

Irene: [lead], angry, loving, has cancer, [black].

MORNINGS AT SEVEN
     Myrtle: [supporting role], sweet, gushy, wishy-washy.

MRS. DALLY HAS A LOVER
     Mrs. Dally: [lead], attractive, passionate, artistic.

MY COUSIN RACHEL
     Rachel: [lead], clever, mysterious, beautiful, materialistic.

'NIGHT MOTHER
     Jessie: [lead], overweight, total lack of self esteem, plans
          to kill herself.

NORMAN CONQUESTS
     Sarah: [supporting role], interfering, proper and righteous.
     Ruth: [supporting role], crisp, cool, realistic, worldly,
          vain, poor eyesight.

NUTS
     Claudia: [lead], outspoken, intelligent, in mental ward.

ONCE A CATHOLIC
     Mother Thomas Aquinas: [supporting role], tall, thin,
          refined.

ON GOLDEN POND
     Chelsea: [supporting role], high strung, resentful, un-
          resolved relationship with father.

OUT OF OUR FATHER'S HOUSE
     Elizabeth Cady Stanton: [lead], women's suffrage movement
          founder, mother of large family.
     "Mother" Mary Jones: [lead], organized labor in 19th cent-
          ury.
     Dr. Anna Howard Shaw: [lead], medical doctor and minister.
     Maria Mitchell: [lead], astronomer, hungry for knowledge.
     Elizabeth Gertrude Stern: [lead], career woman, writer from
          the Jewish ghetto.

A PALM TREE IN A ROSE GARDEN
     Alice: [supporting role], tries to be chic, movie buff.

PATIO
     Jewel: [lead], lots of jewelry, elaborate hair do, easy
          going.
     Pearl: [lead], anxious hostess, wants home to be perfect.

A PHOENIX TOO FREQUENT
     Dynamene: [lead], beautiful, newly-widowed, sorrowful.
     Doto: [lead], servant, practical, earthy, thinks of her
          stomach.

PIZZA
     Grace: [lead], intelligent, creative, not pretty.

PLEASE, NO FLOWERS
    Esther Rubel: [lead], ghost, killed herself jumping off
        bridge.

THE PRIMARY ENGLISH CLASS
    Debbie Westba: [lead], teacher, bright, competent.
    Translator: [supporting role], communicates what others are
        saying.

THE PRIME OF MISS JEAN BRODIE
    Jean Brodie: [lead], powerful, heroic, fanatically romantic,
        progressive ideals.
    Sister Helena: [supporting role], nun, former student
        looking back.
    Miss MacKay: [supporting role], headmistress, angry,
        jealous.

A RAISIN IN THE SUN
    Ruth: [lead], weary, disappointed with life, once pretty.
        [black].

THE RATTLE OF A SIMPLE MAN
    Cyrenne: [lead], intelligent, outspoken, poised, beautiful,
        kind.

REFLECTIONS IN A WINDOW
    Betty: [supporting role], outgoing, stylishly casual,
        responsible.

THE RIMERS OF ELDRITCH
    Evelyn Jackson: [supporting role], mean, nagging, over-
        protective.
    Mavis Johnson: [supporting role], indulgent towards
        daughter.
    Martha Truit: [supporting role], narrow minded gossip.
    Wilma Atkins: [supporting role], narrow minded gossip.
    Cora Groves: [supporting role], owner of cafe, widow with
        young lover.

THE RIVER
    Terry: [lead], direct, positive, broad build but feminine.
    Yvonne: [lead], smaller than Terry, delicate, wistful.

ROADS TO HOME
    Annie: [lead], delicate, dellusional, out of touch with
        reality.

ROOMFUL OF ROSES
    Nancy: [lead], attractive mother, generous, loving, vital.
    Grace: [supporting role], mother, sympathetic, maternal,
        humorous.
    Willamay: [short role], maid.

ROUGE ATOMIQUE
    Wife: [lead], angry possessive, fearful of losing husband.
    Woman: [lead], loving, attractive, believes man loves her
        more.

SAME TIME NEXT YEAR
    Doris: [lead], changes from guilt-ridden, Catholic-reared
        girl who didn't finish high school, to a hippie, then to
        a chic successful business woman.

THE SEA HORSE
    Gertrude: [lead], tired, grubby, overweight, unusually tall.

THE SECRET AFFAIRS OF MILDRED WILD
    Evelyn: [short role], TV hostess, who announces prizes.

SEPARATE CEREMONIES
    Addie: [lead], tall, graceful, humorous, outspoken, defiant.

SHOUT ACROSS THE RIVER
    Mrs. Forsythe: [lead], smartly dressed, nervous, insane.

SISTER MARY IGNATIUS EXPLAINS IT ALL FOR YOU
    Diane Symonds: [supporting role], singer, miserable, angry.
    Philomena Rostovitch: [short role], unwed mother.

6 RMS RIV VU
    Anne: [lead], witty, smart, wife, mother, wants to be
        "hip".
    Janet: [short role], attractive, powerful, active in women's
        movement.

SKIRMISHES
    Jean: [lead], bitter, resentful, childless, tired, exhausted
        and stressed.
    Rita: [lead], mother of three young children, kind, thought-
        ful towards mother.

SLAM THE DOOR SOFTLY
    Nora: [lead], angry, repressed housewife seeks liberation.

SNOWANGEL
    Connie: [lead], joking, kind, prostitute, drinks, vulner-
        able.

SPLIT
    Marge: [supporting role], trendy, "far-out" artist.
    Carol: [supporting role], breaking up with husband, unhappy.
    Jean: [supporting role], artsy, trendy.

STAGE DIRECTIONS
    Ruth: [lead], thin, hawk-like, despairing.

STANDARD SAFETY
> Denise: [lead], depressed, in analysis.
> Andrea: [lead], supporting husband through school.
> Sheila: [supporting role], friend of Denise and Andrea.
> Mary Farrell: [short role], petty, punitive, executive secretary.
> Louella: [short role], embarrassed, publicly exposed secret scribbler.

STEAMING
> Josie: [supporting role], vulgar, kept by lover who beats her, angry, bored, frustrated.
> Dawn: [supporting role], daughter of Mrs. Meadow, humorous food addict, overweight, unrecovered from emotional trauma, immature.
> Nancy: [supporting role], new patron, unsure, nervous, well off, mother, divorced.
> Jane: [supporting role], outgoing, bohemian dress, student, lonely.

STUFFINGS
> Gladys Koontz: [lead], taxidermist, plain, wears glasses, dowdy.

SURPRISE, SURPRISE
> Jeannine: [lead], well balanced, calm, sensible.
> Laurette: [lead], bossy, talks tough.
> Madeline: [lead], feels persecuted, furious, seeking revenge.

TALLEY'S FOLLY
> Sally: [supporting role], attractive, unmarried, embarrassed.

TALKING WITH...
> Fifteen Minutes: [lead], seasoned performer carries on a conversation with the audience wondering what their lives are like.
> Scraps: [lead], kinky comic housewife who lives in a fantasy world of Oz and vacuums the floor wearing a brightly colored patchwork costume based on a character from her fantasy.
> Clear Glass Marbles: [lead], a woman describes how her mother refused to allow a terminal disease to dampen her spirits.
> Audition: [lead], a nervous, desperate, flaky woman is auditioning for a role in a play.
> Rodeo: [lead], a robust rodeo rider sadly describes the changes that are spoiling the rodeo world.
> Dragons: [lead], a woman laboring in childbirth.
> French Fries: [lead], satiric piece about a woman whose favorite food is a hamburger from MacDonald's.
> Marks: [lead], a woman with tatoos covering her body describes her philosophy.

THIS BIRD OF DAWNING SINGETH ALL NIGHT LONG
    Anne Jillett: [lead], frightened, bigoted, patronizing.
      [white].
    Nancy: [lead], stereotyped, bandana, Southern accent.
      [black].

THYMUS VULGARIS
    Evelyn: [lead], garish vivid hair color, likable, practical.

TODAY IS INDEPENDENCE DAY
    Evalyn: [lead], intelligent, sexy, dissatisfied and wants
      more of life.

TOP GIRLS
    Marlene: [lead], powerful, no-nonsense, career minded,
      ambitious, high achiever.
    Isabella Bird: [supporting role], indomitable, world travel-
      er, lived in Edinburgh, 1831-1904.
    Lady Nijo: [supporting role], Japanese courtesan, became
      Buddhist nun and traveled through Japan on foot.
    Dull Gret: [supporting role], from a painting by Brueghel,
      in apron and armour leads a crowd of women.
    Pope Joan: [supporting role], believed to have been pope
      from 854 till 856.
    Patient Griselda: [supporting role], character from Canter-
      bury Tales, the obedient wife.
    Joyce: [supporting role], sister of Marlene, stayed home and
      cared for family, resentful.
    Win: [supporting role], staff member of agency, affair with
      married man, ambitious, hard, dynamic, quick.
    Louise: [short role], client looking for job, conscien-
      tious, hard working.
    Nell: [supporting role], staff of employment agency, tough,
      ambitious, hard.
    Angie: (played by adult), [supporting role], childish, niece
      of Marlene, enthusiastic admiration for Marlene.
    Kit: (played by adult), [supporting role], cohort of Angie,
      troubled, argumentative.
    Mrs. Kidd: [short role], angry, whining, wife of man who
      lost out to Marlene for promotion.
    Waitress: [short role], non speaking.

A TOUCH OF MARBLE
    Helen: [lead], neurotic, hesitant, guarded, fearful, tense.
    Honey: [short role], beautiful, slim, vain, unhappy.
    Miss Carroll: [short role], brisk school administrator.
    Aunt Margaret: [short role], exacerbated nerves, supportive.

TROUBLE IN MIND
    Millie: [supporting role], elegantly dressed, stage per-
      former, unhappy. [black].

THE TWELVE POUND LOOK
    Kate: [lead], self reliant, serene, unassuming, sure of
      herself.

Lady Sims: [supporting role], dutiful, dependent proud, unsure of herself.

TWIGS
Emily: [lead], attractive divorcee courted by moving man.
Celia: [lead], bored by husband's beer drinking sports talk.

TWO O'CLOCK FEEDING
Louise: [lead], well educated, poet, angry, exhausted new mother.

UP THE DOWN STAIRCASE
Beatrice Schachter: [supporting role], experienced teacher, supportive, cynical.

VIVAT ! VIVAT ! REGINIA
Mary, Queen of Scots: [lead], beautiful, brave, emotional.
Queen Elizabeth I: [lead], brilliant, highly disciplined, intellectual.
First Court Lady: [short role].
Second Court Lady: [short role].

A VOICE OF MY OWN
flexible casting: one performer can play several roles covering famous personalities from women's history.

VOICES
Maya: [supporting role], struggling single mother working on her Ph.D.

WAITING FOR THE PARADE
Catherine: [supporting role], practical, lonely, husband away at war.
Marta: [supporting role], timid, angry, persecuted.
Janet: [supporting role], guilty, compulsive, strong, bossy.

WEST SIDE WALTZ
Robin: [supporting role], pretty, has Brooklyn accent, talks in slang, outrageous dress, nutty.

WINE IN THE WILDERNESS
Tommy: [lead], factory worker, uneducated, unsophisticated. [black].

WINGS
Amy: [supporting role], therapist, kind, professional, group instructor.

WOMANSPEAK
Contemporary Woman: [lead], central figure who converses with women from the past.
Abigail Adams: [supporting role], writer, scholar, advocate of women's rights, lived during American revolution, wife of John Adams.

Sojourner Truth: [supporting role], black slave, eloquent
    spokesperson for civil rights circa 1850.
Harriet Beecher Stowe: [supporting role], abolitionist,
    highly influential author of Uncle Tom's Cabin which
    exposed the evils of slavery.
Anna Carroll: [supporting role], researcher, author of
    Tennessee Plan which helped the North to win the Civil
    war.
Susan B. Anthony: [supporting role], organizer of women's
    suffrage campaign.
Victoria Woodhull: [supporting role], advocate for equal
    rights, abortion, and free love, ran for U.S. president.
Mother Jones: [supporting role], courageous organizer of the
    United Mine Workers.
Adelita: [supporting role], soldier in New Mexico in 1913,
    follower of Pancho Villa.
Margaret Sanger: [supporting role], leader of the birth
    control movement in 1917.
Eleanor Roosevelt: [supporting role], advocate for social
    causes, writer, lecturer, wife of Franklin Roosevelt.
Emma Goldman: [supporting role], anarchist, activist.

THE WOODS
    Ruth: [lead], outgoing, convivial, strong willed, out spo-
       ken.

A YOUNG LADY OF PROPERTY
    Mrs. Leighton: [short role], warm, attractive, gracious.

Character Ages 40 to 50

ABSURD PERSON SINGULAR
    Marion: [supporting role], drinking problem, the wife of the
       boss.

AGNES OF GOD
    Mother Miriam Ruth: [lead], mystical nun, defends the
       church.

AN ALMOST PERFECT PERSON
    Irene Porter: [lead], vital, witty, idealistic attorney
       running for Congress, widow.

THE AMERICAN DREAM
    Mommy: [lead], bossy, cruel.
    Mrs. Baker: [supporting role], arrogant, busy, committee
       member.

AND MISS REARDON DRINKS A LITTLE
    Catherine: [lead], judgmental, argumentative, has drinking
       problem.

Ceil Adams: [lead], successful school administrator, married man her sister loved.
Anna Reardon: [lead], obsessed with death, emotional crisis.
Fleur Steen: [supporting role], tense, trite teacher.
Mrs. Pentrano: [short role], comic, sells cosmetics, malaprop.

AUNTIE MAME
Auntie Mame: [lead], courageous, adventuresome, spirited.
Vera: [supporting role], comic, actor, heavy drinker.
Norah Muldoon: [short role], spunky nanny.

THE AU PAIR MAN
Mrs. Rogers: [lead], stately, educated, well-to-do, very British.

THE AUTOGRAPH HOUND
Lila: [lead], dumpy, hair askew, frumpy, energetic, tyrannical.

A BAD YEAR FOR TOMATOES
Myra Marlowe: [lead], witty, successful, fed up with job.
Cora Gump: [supporting role], small town, friendly, well meaning, trite.
Reba Harper: [supporting role], gossip, conventional, provincial.
Willa Mae Wilcox: [supporting role], furtive, suspected of being a witch.

BEAUTY AND THE BEAST
Mrs. C. Crunch: [lead], ancient witch, gruff, practical, comic.
Madame Suzanne: [supporting role], French fairy, rouged, extravagant.

LES BELLES SOEURS
Germaine: [lead], gloating, coarse, vulgar, abrasive.
Rose: [lead], narrow minded, bigoted, judgmental, prudish.
Gabrielle: [supporting role], nuts about contests, common, bossy.
Therese: [supporting role], stuck-up, smug, husband just got a raise.
Marie-Ange: [supporting role], overworked housewife, jealous, bitter.
Yvette: [supporting role], obsessed with daughter's wedding, honeymoon.

THE BICYCLE RIDERS
Patsy: [lead], whimsical, sprite, clown costumed.

BLACK GIRL
Mama Rosie: [supporting role], tall, powerful, authoritarian, [black].

BLOOD PHOTO
    Angela Benedetto: [lead], huge earthy mother, dominates
        family, shrewd, cunning.

BONJOUR LA BONJOUR
    Lucienne: [supporting role], snobbish, status conscious,
        married to Englishman.

BRINGING IT ALL BACK HOME
    Mother: [supporting role], shallow, out of touch with her
        feelings.

BRONTOSAURUS
    Dealer: [lead], well dressed, cynical, wise cracking,
        brittle.

BUTTERFLIES ARE FREE
    Mrs. Baker: [supporting role], Scarsdale matron, well-
        dressed, worried about blind son.

CALIFORNIA SUITE
    Hannah: [lead], sophisticated, wants custody of her
        daughter.
    Millie: [supporting role], wife who catches her husband
        cheating.
    Diana: [lead], expensively dressed, award nominee.
    Beth: [supporting role], comic, tennis playing vacationer.
    Gert: [supporting role], comic, tennis playing vacationer.

CALM DOWN MOTHER
    any of characters.

THE CHALK GARDEN
    Madrigal: [lead], intense, neat, contained, calm, humorless.
    Second applicant: [short role], small, energetic, nervous.

CHILDREN OF A LESSER GOD
    Mrs. Norman: [supporting role], mother of deaf woman,
        bitter, resigned.

CHOCOLATE CAKE
    Delia: [lead], likable, crude, enjoys pinball, noise, and
        action.

CLARA'S OLE MAN
    Miss Famie: [short role], alcoholic neighbor, thin.

CLOTHES FOR A SUMMER HOTEL
    Zelda: [lead], once popular Southern belle, now in asylum,
        fiery.

THE COAL DIAMOND
    Lena: [lead], the boss, wears girdle, pumps, and rayon print
        dress.

COME INTO THE GARDEN, MAUD
    Anna-Mary: [supporting role], snobbish, dressed expensively,
        petty.
    Maude: [supporting role], sophisticated, royalty, individ-
        ualistic.

CONFESSIONS OF A FEMALE DISORDER
    Evelyn: [short role], depressed housewife, next door
        neighbor.

THE CORRUPTERS
    Prison Guard: [short role].

A COUPLA WHITE CHICKS
    Maude Mix: [lead], typical New York suburban housewife,
        comic.
    Hannah Mae Bindler: [lead], newly arrived wife from Texas,
        comic.

THE CURIOUS SAVAGE
    Lily Belle: [supporting role], vain, self-assured, harsh,
        stepdaughter.

THE DANCERS
    Elizabeth: [supporting role], mother, worries about what
        others think.
    Mrs. Davis: [short role], mother, pleased.

THE DARK OF THE MOON AND THE FULL
    Helen: [supporting role], stout, strong, cheerful, peasant-like.

    Loretta: [short role], efficient, serious, strained.

THE DARNING NEEDLE
    Betty: [lead], tough, abrasive, uneducated, simple, coarse.
    Ida: [lead], dressmaker, psychic, astrologer, affable.

A DELICATE BALANCE
    Claire: [supporting role], alcoholic, outspoken, warm,
        vulgar.

DENTIST AND PATIENT
    Anybody: [lead], naive, dentist, honest, gullible.
    Anybody else: [lead], unscrupulous patient, stingy, million-
        aire.

DESIGN FOR LIVING
    Miss Hodge: [short role], untidy, comic servant.

THE DRAPES COME
    Mrs. Fiers: [lead], mother, likable, kind, meek, then
        changes to domineering, nasty, abrasive.

THE EFFECT OF GAMMA RAYS
    Beatrice: [lead], angry, resentful, unkempt, widow, strug-
        gling.

THE EYE OF THE BEHOLDER
    Jane: [lead], slim, fair, intellectual, artistic style cool
        and classical.
    Bella: [lead], heavy set, dark, emotional, artistic
        style intense, free, loose, abandoned.
    Leona: [supporting role], model, attractive, opinionated,
        joins in conversation.

FINISHING TOUCHES
    Katy: [lead], literate, quick-witted, sarcastic, dowdy.

FIRST MONDAY IN OCTOBER
    Ruth Loomis: [lead], newly-appointed justice of the Supreme
        Court, quick witted, high moral principles, politically
        conservative.

FOR THE USE OF THE HALL
    Charlotte: [lead], tall, graceful, chic, penniless, bitter.

FORTY CARATS
    Ann Stanley: [lead], successful real estate broker, elegant.

FUNNYHOUSE OF A NEGRO
    Queen Victoria: [supporting role], back turned to audience,
        wears a white mask, never moves.
    Duchess of Hapsburg: [supporting role], back turned to
        audience, wears a white mask, never moves.
    Landlady: [supporting role], tall, thin.

GIFT OF MURDER!
    Flavia: [supporting role], rival performer, tall, arresting,
        vain, acid, biting wit.
    Nurse: [supporting role], ageless, unlimited curiosity,
        secretly resentful, impersonator.

THE GINGERBREAD LADY
    Evy: [lead], glamorous, nervous, just back from sanatarium.
    Toby: [supporting role], friend of Evy, pretty, well-
        dressed.

GOD SAYS THERE IS NO PETER OTT
    Avis: [lead], carelessly dressed, drinker, tough, whimsical.
    Marcia: [short role], narrow minded mother, smartly dressed.

GOLDA
    Lou: middle aged, [short role], also plays Clara middle
        aged, and DP.
    Mother: middle aged, [short role], also plays third witness,
        Sarile middle aged, DP.

GOODBYE MY FANCY
    Agatha Reed: [lead], successful, tough, idealistic, con-
        gresswoman.
    Ellen Griswold: [supporting role], former beauty, plump,
        superficial.

HAY FEVER
    Judith Bliss: [lead], glamorous, eccentric, extravagant.

HOT L BALTIMORE
    Mrs. Oxenham: [short role], no-nonsense desk clerk.

HOW THE OTHER HALF LOVES
    Fiona Foster: [supporting role], well-off, smart, sophis-
        ticated.

I AM A CAMERA
    Fraulein: [supporting role], broad, lusty humor, self-pity,
        intimate.
    Mrs. Watson-Courtneidge: [short role], genteel, British
        matron.

I JUST WANTED SOMEONE TO KNOW
    figures from labor history, [short roles].

I OUGHT TO BE IN PICTURES
    Steffy: [supporting role], single mother dating single
        father, neglected and expected to wait around for him.

THE KILLING OF SISTER GEORGE
    June: [lead], heavy set, plays kind do-gooder on TV show, in
        real life smokes cigars, swears, drinks gin.
    Mrs. Mercy Croft: [supporting role], business-like staff for
        BBC radio.

KILLINGS ON THE LAST LINE
    Juba: [supporting role], Bahamian, sings song in play.
    Quashie: [supporting role], Bahamian, has leg in cast.

THE KNIGHT AT THE TWELFTH SAUCER
    Rose: [supporting role], overweight, obsessed with food,
        still delicate.
    Tillie: [supporting role], tired, frail.

LADIES AT THE ALAMO
    Dede Cooper: [lead], charming, gutsy, intense, individual-
        ist.
    Bella Gardner: [lead], calculating, drinker, small-time
        star.
    Joanne Remington: [supporting role], powerful, repressed
        aggressions.
    Shirley Fuller: [supporting role], award nominee, very en-
        ergetic, active.

THE LADIES SHOULD BE IN BED
    Maggie: [lead], noisy, theatrical, vicious, bigot, drinking.
    Charlotte: [lead], plump, caustic, sexually explicit talk.
    Elinore: [supporting role], unmarried, lives with elderly
        mother.
    Maureen: [supporting role], nurse, stable, quiet, helpful,
        soft.
    Lucille: [supporting role], domestic worker, [black].

THE LADY FROM DUBUQUE
    Elizabeth: [supporting role], wise, mysterious, under-
        standing.

LADY OF LARKSPUR LOTION
    Mrs. Hardwicke-Moore: [lead], prostitute, fantasies of ele-
        gance.

LADYHOUSE BLUES
    Liz: [supporting role], sex appeal, plain, rustic, un-
        educated.

THE LARK
    Joan's mother: [short role], loving, supportive.
    Yolande: [short role], mother of Queen, worldly, realistic.

THE LAST OF MRS. LINCOLN
    Mary Todd Lincoln: [lead], tragic, compassionate, cour-
        ageous.
    Lizzie Keckley: [supporting role], former slave, servant,
        [black].

A LATE SNOW
    Margo: [supporting role], famous writer, recluse, self con-
        tained.

LATER
    Kate: [lead], bossy, stubborn, argumentative, unpredictable.

LET ME HEAR YOU WHISPER
    Miss Moray: [lead], uptight, brisk, efficient, mean.
    Dr. Crocus: [short role], performs weird experiments on
        animals.
    Ms. Fridge: [short role], assistant, not very bright, obe-
        dient.
    Danielle: [supporting role], talky janitor, easy going,
        irresponsible.

LETTERS HOME
    Aurelia: [lead], Sylvia's mother, loving supportive.

LOOK AWAY
    Elizabeth Keckley: [lead], dressmaker, former slave,
        [black].

A LOVELY SUNDAY FOR CREVE COEUR
    Bodey: [lead], German, hard-of-hearing, plump, simple, com-
        mon.

LOVERS
    Hanna: [supporting role], caught between husband and
        mother's dominance.

LOVERS AND OTHER STRANGERS
    Bea: [lead], old fashioned, stubborn.

LUANN HAMPTON
    LuAnn: [lead], first act: wholesome cheerleader second act:
        10 years later, hardened beauty operator; third act:
        another 10 years, matronly beautiful, lively, works for
        welcome wagon.
    Claudine; [supporting role], stout, widowed complains.

MAJOR BARBARA
    Mrs. Baines: [short role], Salvation Army Commissioner,
        earnest.

A MEMBER OF THE WEDDING
    Berenice Sadie Brown: [lead], family cook, loving, wise,
        motherly, [black].

MISS MARGARIDA'S WAY
    Miss Margarida: [lead], prototype of totalitarian dictator.

NEVIS MOUNTAIN DEW
    Everelda: [supporting role], reserved, sour, righteous,
        self-sacrificing.
    Zepora: [supporting role], lively, fun-loving, kind, drinks.
    Billie: [supporting role], loyal to incapacitated husband.

OLD TIMES
    Kate: [lead], introvert, dreamer.
    Anna: [lead], outgoing, friendly, gregarious.

ONCE A CATHOLIC
    Mother Peter: [supporting role], nun, tall, stout, venomous
        teacher.

ON GOLDEN POND
    Chelsea: [supporting role], resentful, unresolved relation-
        ship with her father.

OPAL SERIES
    Opal: [lead], zany, optimistic, raunchy, coarse and common.
    Rosie: [supporting role], caustic, bitter, her husband left
        10 years ago.
    Queenie: [supporting role], flamboyant, pretentious,
        snobbish, greedy.

OUT OF OUR FATHER'S HOUSE
> Elizabeth Cady Stanton: [lead], women's suffrage movement
> founder, mother.
> "Mother" Mary Jones: [lead], organized labor in 19th cent-
> ury.
> Dr. Anna Howard Shaw: [lead], medical doctor and minister.
> Maria Mitchell: [lead], astronomer, hungry for knowledge.
> Elizabeth Gertrude Stern: [lead], career woman, writer from
> the Jewish ghetto.

A PERFECT ANALYSIS GIVEN FOR A PARROT
> Bessie: [lead], heavy set, garishly dressed.
> Flora: [lead], very thin, garishly dressed.

PORCH
> Lucille: [lead], old-fashioned swim suit, manipulated by
> mother.

THE PRIME OF MISS JEAN BRODIE
> Jean Brodie: [lead], powerful, heroic, individualistic,
> prideful, romantic, progressive ideals.
> Miss MacKay: [supporting role], headmistress, brisk, con-
> servative, angry and jealous.

THE RIMERS OF ELDRITCH
> Nelly Windrod: [supporting role], coarse, unpleasant,
> bullies elderly mother.
> Mavis Johnson: [supporting role], mother, indulgent towards
> daughter.
> Martha Truit: [supporting role], narrow minded gossip.
> Wilma Atkins: [supporting role], narrow minded gossip.
> Cora Groves: [supporting role], owner of cafe, widow with
> young lover.

ROADS TO HOME
> Mabel: [lead], friendly, warm, from small town, supportive.
> Vonnie: [lead], neighbor, kind, Southerner, friendly,
> folksy.

ROOM FOR ONE WOMAN
> Lil: [supporting role], overworked, impatient and resentful.

ROUGE ATOMIQUE
> Wife: [lead], angry, possessive, fearful of losing husband.
> Woman: [lead], loving, attractive, believes man loves her
> more.

THE SAND CASTLE
> Irene: [supporting role], mother, quiet, college teacher,
> widow.

SEASCAPE
> Nancy: [lead], friendly, enthusiastic, zest for life.
> Sarah: [lead], a lizard-like reptile from the sea.

THE SECRET AFFAIRS OF MILDRED WILD
     Mildred: [lead], fanatic about movies, garish.
     Berthe: [supporting role], energetic, prudishly dressed,
         efficiency nut.
     Miss Manley: [supporting role], TV crew, slick, assertive,
         tough.

SEPARATE CEREMONIES
     Carrie: [lead], eldest child, responsible, surviving.

SISTER MARY IGNATIUS EXPLAINS IT ALL FOR YOU
     Sister Mary Ignatius: [lead], ridiculous, out of touch, not
         very bright, mindlessly recites church dogma.

SOMETHING UNSPOKEN
     Miss Grace Lancaster: [supporting role], thin, subservient.

STANDARD SAFETY
     Mrs. MacIntosh: [short role], personnel director, mean,
         petty.

STEAMING
     Violet: [supporting role], proprietor of steam bath,
         helpful, maternal.

STRING
     Mrs. Beverly: [lead], civic minded, hard worker, conscien-
         tious, [black].
     Mrs. Rogers: [lead], conservative dresser, uppity, bossy,
         [black].

SUNSET/SUNRISE
     Louise: [lead], compulsive, angry about husband's philan-
         dering.
     Gem: [lead], successful businesswoman, competent, newly
         married.
      Dianne: [supporting role], neighbor, energetic, com-
         passionate, divorced.

TALKING WITH...
     Fifteen Minutes: [lead], seasoned performer carries
         on a conversation with the audience wondering what their
         lives are like.
     Scraps: [lead], kinky comic housewife who lives in
         a fantasy world of Oz and vacuums the floor wearing a
         brightly colored patchwork costume based on a character
         from her fantasy.
     Clear Glass Marbles: [lead], a woman describes how her
         mother refused to allow a terminal disease to dampen
         her spirits.
     Rodeo: [lead], a robust rodeo rider sadly describes the
         changes that are spoiling the rodeo world.
     Lamps: [lead], a woman in later years describes how she used
         lamps to fill the voids.

French Fries: [lead], satiric piece about a woman whose
favorite food is a hamburger from MacDonald's.
Marks: [lead], a woman with tatoos covering her body
describes her philosophy.

TOP GIRLS
Marlene: 30s, [lead], powerful, no nonsense, career minded,
ambitious, high achiever.
Isabella Bird: [supporting role], 19th century individ-
ualist, traveled extensively from 40 to 70 years of age.
Lady Nijo: [supporting role], Japanese courtesan, became
Buddhist nun and traveled through Japan on foot.
Dull Gret: [supporting role], from a painting by Brueghel,
in apron and armour leads a crowd of women.
Pope Joan: [supporting role], believed to have been pope in
854 till 856.
Patient Griselda: [supporting role], character from Canter-
bury Tales, the obedient wife.
Joyce: 30s, [supporting role], sister of Marlene, stayed
home, cared for family, resentful.
Win: [supporting role], staff member of agency, affair with
married man, ambitious, hard, dynamic, quick.
Louise: 40s, [short role], client looking for job, conscien-
tious, hard working.
Nell: [supporting role], staff of employment agency, tough,
ambitious, hard.
Angie: 16, (played by adult), [supporting role], childish,
niece of Marlene, enthusiastic admirer of Marlene.
Kit: 12, (played by adult), [supporting role], cohort of
Angie, troubled, argumentative.
Mrs. Kidd: 40s-50s, [short role], angry, whining, wife of
man who lost out to Marlene for promotion.
Jeanine: 20, [short role], seeking a better job, not sure of
what she wants, moderate skills.
Shona: 21, [short role], client seeking job, brash, cheeky,
fabricates job experience.
Waitress: [short role], non speaking.

A TOUCH OF MARBLE
Miss Carroll: [short role], brisk school administrator.
Aunt Margaret: [short role], teacher, exacerbated nerves,
bitter.

TROUBLE IN MIND
Wiletta: [lead], savy, stage performer, speaks mind, good
singing voice, [black].

THE TWELVE POUND LOOK
Kate: [lead], self reliant, unassuming, sure of herself,
serene.
Lady Sims: [supporting role], dutiful, dependent, proud,
uncertain.

TWIGS
>   Dorothy: [lead], suburban,   celebrating 25th wedding anni-
>   versary.

TWO O'CLOCK FEEDING
>   Marie: [supporting role], experienced mother of four,
>   active, under pressure, drinks.

VERONICA'S ROOM
>   The woman: [lead], changes identities,   mysterious, insane.

A VERY RICH WOMAN
>   Edith: [supporting role], pretty, chic, greedy, pretentious,
>   dishonest.
>   Ursala: [supporting role], chic, artificial, shallow, self-centered.

A VOICE OF MY OWN
>   flexible casting- one performer can play several roles
>   covering famous personalities from women's history.

VOICES
>   Grace: [supporting role], feels useless since her children
>   have grown up and left home.

WOMANSPEAK
>   Contemporary Woman: [lead], central figure who con-
>   verses with women from the past.
>   Abigail Adams: [supporting role], writer, scholar, advocate
>   of women's rights, lived during American revolution, wife
>   of John Adams.
>   Sojourner Truth: [supporting role], black slave, eloquent
>   spokesperson for civil rights circa 1850.
>   Harriet Beecher Stowe: [supporting role], abolitionist,
>   highly influential author of <u>Uncle</u> <u>Tom's</u> <u>Cabin</u> which
>   exposed the evils of slavery.
>   Anna Carroll: [supporting role], researcher, author of
>   Tennessee Plan which helped the North to win the Civil
>   war.
>   Susan B. Anthony: [supporting role], organizer of women's
>   suffrage campaign.
>   Victoria Woodhull: [supporting role], advocate for equal
>   rights, abortion, and free love, ran for U.S. president.
>   Mother Jones: [supporting role], courageous organizer of the
>   United Mine Workers.
>   Adelita: [supporting role], soldier in New Mexico in 1913,
>   follower of Pancho Villa.
>   Margaret Sanger: [supporting role], leader of the birth
>   control movement in 1917.
>   Eleanor Roosevelt: [supporting role], advocate for social
>   causes, writer, lecturer, wife of Franklin Roosevelt.
>   Emma Goldman: [supporting role], anarchist, activist.

A YOUNG LADY OF PROPERTY
      Miss Gert: [supporting role], tall, good looking, solid.
      Minna: [supporting role], thin, strong, domestic worker.
         [black].
      Miss Martha Davenport: [short role], giddy post office
         clerk.

Character Ages 50 to 60

AGNES OF GOD
      Dr. Martha Livingstone: [lead], psychiatrist, former Catho-
         lic.
      Mother Miriam Ruth: [lead], mystical nun, defends the
         church.

AND
      Ruth: [lead], repressed anger and resentment, on the surface
         tidy and well behaved, has just murdered husband.

AND IF THAT MOCKING BIRD DON'T SING
      Darlene: [supporting role], waitress, tough, kind, loyal.
         [black].

AND MISS REARDON DRINKS A LITTLE
      Mrs. Pentrano: [short role], comic, sells cosmetics, mala-
         prop.

AUGUSTUS
      Duchess: [lead], matriarch, imposing, elegant, proud, grand.

AUNTIE MAME
      Doris Upson: [short role], snobbish, narrow minded, subur-
         banite.

THE AU PAIR MAN
      Mrs. Rogers: [lead], stately, well educated, accomplished,
         British.

A BAD YEAR FOR TOMATOES
      Myra Marlowe: [lead], witty, successful TV star, fed up with
         job, needing rest.
      Cora Gump: [supporting role], small town, friendly, well
         meaning, trite.
      Reba Harper: [supporting role], gossip, conventional, pro-
         vincial.
      Willa Mae Wilcox: [supporting role], furtive, tiny, in-
         terested in the occult, suspected of being a witch.

BAG LADY
      Clara: [lead], shabbily dressed, big overcoat, mutters to
         self.

BEAUTY AND THE BEAST
    Mrs. C. Crunch: [lead], witch, gruff, practical, comic.
    Madame Suzanne: [supporting role], fairy, French accent,
        extravagant.

BEDROOM FARCE
    Delia: [supporting role], cranky, complaining.

BELL, BOOK, AND CANDLE
    Miss Holroyd: [supporting role], eccentric aunt, a witch.

THE BELLE OF AMHERST
    Emily: [lead], looks younger than her years, poet, eccentric
        recluse, unhappy victim of life.

LES BELLES SOEURS
    Angeline: [supporting role], lively, risque, night club
        patron.
    Rheauna: [supporting role], poor health, prudish, narrow
        minded.

BERTHE
    Berthe: [lead], garish, wears wildly shaped, glittery blue
        plastic glasses, worldly, crude, disappointed.

BLACK GIRL
    Mu' Dear: [short role], grandmother, thin, short, [black].
    Mama Rosie: [supporting role], tall, powerful, author-
        itarian, [black].

BLOOD PHOTO
    Angela Benedetto: [lead], earthy mother, dominates family,
        shrewd, cunning.

BOSEMAN AND LENA
    Lena: [lead], tired, burdened, had hard life, [black].

BONJOUR LA BONJOUR
    Albertine: [supporting role], TV addict, cranky aunt.
    Charlotte: [supporting role], complains about health,
        suspicious, vindictive aunt.

BRINGING IT ALL BACK HOME
    Mother: [supporting role], shallow, out of touch with her
        feelings, overly patriotic.

BUTTERFLIES ARE FREE
    Mrs. Baker: [supporting role], well dressed, Scarsdale
        matron, worried about blind son.

CASTLE IN THE VILLAGE
    Mrs. Goldfine: [supporting role], landlady, nervous, "out of
        breath".

CATSPLAY
　　Mousie: [short role], neighbor, shy, plain, loyal.

THE CHALK GARDEN
　　Third applicant: [short role], great bearing, haughty.

CHILDREN OF A LESSER GOD
　　Mrs. Norman: [supporting role], mother of deaf woman,
　　　bitter, resigned.

CLARA'S OLE MAN
　　Miss Famie: [short role], alcoholic neighbor, thin, [black].

CLOTHES FOR A SUMMER HOTEL
　　Zelda: [lead], once popular, now in asylum, fiery, unkempt.

THE COAL DIAMOND
　　Lena: [lead], the boss, wears girdle, pumps, and rayon print
　　　dress.

THE COCKTAIL PARTY
　　Julia: [supporting role], worldly socialite, poised, sophis-
　　　ticated.

COME INTO THE GARDEN, MAUD
　　Anna-Mary: [supporting role], snobbish, dressed expensively,
　　　petty.

COMPANIONS OF THE FIRE
　　Woman: [lead], fun-loving, wears an obvious wig, very fat.
　　　[black].

A COUPLA WHITE CHICKS SITTING AROUND TALKING
　　Maude Mix: [lead], typical suburban housewife, comic.
　　Hannah Mae Bindler: [lead], housewife from Texas, comic.

CRABDANCE
　　Sadie Golden: [lead], tall, sagging, coarse, blunt, unique.

CROWN MATRIMONIAL
　　Queen Mary: [lead], stately monarch, proper.
　　Lady Arlie [supporting role], lady in waiting, confidant,
　　　loyal friend.

THE CURIOUS SAVAGE
　　Mrs. Paddy: [supporting role], eccentric artist, stout,
　　　aggressive.

THE DARNING NEEDLE
　　Betty: [lead], tough, practical, abrasive, uneducated, sim-
　　　ple.
　　Ida: [lead], dressmaker, psychic, affable, astrologer.

A DELICATE BALANCE
    Agnes: [lead], elegant, tightly controlled emotions, cool.
    Claire: [supporting role], alcoholic, out-spoken, warm,
        vulgar.
    Edna: [supporting role], freaking out with fear.

DENTIST AND PATIENT
    Anybody: [lead], naive dentist, honest, gullible chump.
    Anybody else: [lead], millionaire, crafty, unscrupulous,
        stingy.

DESIGN FOR LIVING
    Miss Hodge: [short role], untidy, comic servant.

DUCHESSE DE LANGAIS
    La Duchesse: [lead], retired prostitute, French, lively, has
        had eventful life, sexually explicit, coarse.

THE EYE OF THE BEHOLDER
    Jane: [lead], slim, fair, intellectual, artistic style
        cool and classical.
    Bella: [lead], heavy set, dark, emotional, artistic
        style intense, free, loose, abandoned.
    Leona: [supporting role], model, attractive, opinionated,
        joins in conversation.

FIRST BREEZE OF SUMMER
    Aunt Edna: [supporting role], daughter of Gremmar, earthy,
        lively, [black].
    Hattie: [supporting role], daughter-in-law, tease, [black].

FIRST MONDAY IN OCTOBER
    Ruth Loomis: [lead], newly appointed justice of the Supreme
        Court, quick witted, high moral principles, politically
        conservative.

THE FLOUNDER COMPLEX
    Woman: [lead], sneaky, conniving, bigoted, paranoid.

FORTY CARATS
    Mrs. Latham: [supporting role], youthful for age, elegant,
        wealthy.
    Mrs. Margolin: [short role], secretary.

THE FROGS
    Mrs. Tupper: [lead], overweight, critical but affable.

FUNNYHOUSE OF A NEGRO
    Queen Victoria: [supporting role], back turned to audience,
        wears white mask.
    Duchess of Hapsburg: [supporting role], back turned to
        audience, wears white mask.
    Landlady: [supporting role], tall, thin, long monologue.

GETTING OUT
    Mother: [supporting role], taxi-driver, withholds love.
    School principal: [short role].

GIFT OF MURDER!
    Stella: [lead], famous star, jagged nerves, temper tantrums,
        on the wagon, sympathetic.
    Flavia: [supporting role], Stella's rival, tall, vain,
        arresting, caustic.
    Nurse: [supporting role], impersonator, secret grudge, en-
        ergetic, curious, ageless.
    Wimpie: [supporting role], efficient housekeeper, outspoken.

GOLDA
    Golda: 50s, [lead], determined, idealistic, formidable ad-
        ministrator, compassionate.
    Lou: middle aged, [short role], also plays Clara middle
        aged, and DP.
    Mother: middle aged, [short role], also plays third witness,
        Sarile middle aged, DP.

GOODBYE MY FANCY
    Grace Woods: [supporting role], top notch secretary, very
        knowledgeable.

HAY FEVER
    Judith Bliss: [lead], glamorous, eccentric, extravagant.

I AM A CAMERA
    Mrs. Watson-Courtneidge: [short role], genteel, British ma-
        tron.

I JUST WANTED SOMEONE TO KNOW
    Figures from labor history: [short roles].

I LOST A PAIR OF GLOVES YESTERDAY
    An Actress: [lead], monologue, tired, despairing, flashes of
        vivaciousness.

THE INDEPENDENT FEMALE
    Matilda Pennybank: [supporting role], mother of Gloria,
        petty, trite, firmly believes that women should be
        subservient to men.

IN THE DESERT OF MY SOUL
    Ma: [lead], tough, foul-mouthed, blunt, but caring.

JACOB'S LADDER
    Annie: [short role], outspoken, merry widow, motherly, sup-
        portive.

THE KILLING OF SISTER GEORGE
    June: [lead], heavy-set, plays kind do-gooder on TV show, in
        real life smokes cigars, uses generous amounts of profan-

ity, drinks gin, and temperamentally dominates her les-
bian lover.
Mrs. Mercy Croft: [supporting role], business-like, staff at
BBC radio.

KILLINGS ON THE LAST LINE
Mrs. Starkey: [supporting role], defiant, kookie mother.
[black].

THE KNIGHT AT THE TWELFTH SAUCER
Rose: [supporting role], overweight, obsessed with food,
still delicate.
Tillie: [supporting role], tired, frail.

THE LADY FROM DUBUQUE
Elizabeth: [supporting role], wise, mysterious stranger,
understanding.

LADY OF LARKSPUR LOTION
Mrs. Wire: [supporting role], blunt, unkempt, overweight,
landlady.

THE LAST OF MRS. LINCOLN
Mary Todd Lincoln: [lead], kind, compassionate, courageous,
tragic.

LATER
Molly: [lead], mourning for husband, edgy, has ulcer, lit-
erate, well educated.

LEMONADE
Mabel: [lead], affluent, expensively dressed.
Edith: [lead], a little smaller than Mabel physically, af-
fluent.

LET ME HEAR YOU WHISPER
Helen: [lead], cleaning lady, feeds stray animals, tender
hearted.
Miss Moray: [lead], uptight, brisk, efficient, mean, super-
visor.
Dr. Crocus: [short role], mean, performs weird experiments
on animals.
Ms. Fridge: [short role], assistant to Dr. Crocus, not very
bright, obedient.
Danielle: [supporting role], talky janitor, easy going,
irresponsible.

LETTERS HOME
Aurelia: [lead], mother of poet, loving supportive.

LOOK AWAY
Mary Todd Lincoln: [lead], embittered by a life of tragedies.
Elizabeth Keckley: [lead], dressmaker, former slave.
[black].

A LOVELY SUNDAY FOR CREVE COEUR
    Miss Gluck: [short role], humorous, German speaking.

LOVERS AND OTHER STRANGERS
    Bea: [lead], old fashioned, stubborn.

THE LOVES OF CASS MCGUIRE
    Alice: [short role], sister-in-law, expensively dressed.

MAJOR BARBARA
    Lady Britomart: [supporting role], brusque, independent,
        liberal.

MAUD GONNE SAYS NO TO THE POET
    Maud: [lead], colorful, extravagant, articulate, maudlin.

THE MIDNIGHT CALLER
    Mrs. Crawford: [supporting role], proprietor of rooming
        house, motherly.

MISS MARGARIDA'S WAY
    Miss Margarida: [lead], a prototype of a totalitarian dicta-
        tor.

MY SISTER IN THIS HOUSE
    Madame Danzard: [lead], domineering, stingy, petty, cruel.

'NIGHT MOTHER
    Thelma: [lead], conventional, ordinary, talkative, recently
        widowed.

NUTS
    Rose: [supporting role], worried about her daughter fighting
        legal battle.

OH DAD, POOR DAD
    Madame Rosepettle: [lead], overpowering, paranoid, puritan-
        ical, domineering, obsessive.

ONCE A CATHOLIC
    Mother Peter: [supporting role], nun, tall, stout, angry,
        venomous teacher.

OPAL SERIES
    Opal: [lead], zany, optimistic, raunchy, coarse, common.
    Rosie: [supporting role], caustic, bitter, her husband left
        her 10 years ago.
    Velma: [supporting role], daughter, mean, aggressive, large.
    Queenie: [supporting role], flamboyant, snobbish, greedy,
        underhanded.

OPENING NIGHT
    Fanny Ellis: [lead], clever, star, tough trouper, alcoholic.

OUT OF OUR FATHER'S HOUSE
    Elizabeth Cady Stanton: [lead], women's suffrage movement founder, mother of large family.
    Maria Mitchell: [lead], astronomer, hungry for knowledge.
    "Mother" Mary Jones: [lead], organizer of labor.
    Dr. Anna Howard Shaw: [lead], medical doctor and minister.
    Elizabeth Gertrude Stern: [lead], career woman, writer from the Jewish ghetto.

A PALM TREE IN A ROSE GARDEN
    Rose Frobisher: [lead], grandiose, Hollywood fan, plump.
    Mona: [supporting role], large, heavy-set, used to work in films.

PIZZA
    Lena: [lead], boisterous, generous, superstitious, possessive, overprotective.
    Sadie: [supporting role], narrow minded busy-body, friend of Lena.

PLEASE, NO FLOWERS
    Mrs. Hirshman: [short role], well dressed, heavy set, crabby, wife of boss.

THE PRIME OF MISS JEAN BRODIE
    Miss MacKay: [supporting role], headmistress of school, angry, jealous.

THE RIMERS OF ELDRITCH
    Nelly Windrod: [supporting role], coarse, unpleasant, mean, bullies elderly mother.

ROUGE ATOMIQUE
    Wife: [lead], angry possessive, fearful of losing husband.
    Woman: [lead], loving, attractive, believes man loves her more.

SARAH AND THE SAX
    Sarah: [lead], cheerful, lonely, talkative, plump, conventional, traditional.

SEASCAPE
    Nancy: [lead], friendly, enthusiastic, zest for life.
    Sarah: [lead], a lizard-like reptile from the sea.

THE SECRET AFFAIRS OF MILDRED WILD
    Mildred: [lead], fanatic about movies, bright hair and make-up, drab dress.
    Berthe: [supporting role], energetic, prudishly dressed, efficiency nut.
    Helen: [supporting role], angry sister-in-law of Mildred.
    Sister Cecelia: [short role], nun.

SISTER MARY IGNATIUS EXPLAINS IT ALL FOR YOU
    Sister Mary Ignatius: [lead], not very bright, ridiculous,
        comic. dressed in old fashioned habit, mindlessly recites
        church doctrines, out of touch.

STANDARD SAFETY
    Mrs. MacIntosh: [short role], personnel director, nasty and
        mean.

STOOP
    First woman: [lead], heavy set, resigned.
    Second woman: [lead], thin, resigned.

STRING
    Mrs. Beverly: [lead], civic minded, hard worker, conscien-
        tious, [black].
    Mrs. Rogers: [lead], conservative, superior, uppity, bossy,
        [black].

TALKING WITH
    Clear Glass Marbles: [lead], a woman describes how her
        mother refused to allow a terminal disease to dampen
        her spirits.
    Lamps: [lead], a woman in later years describes how she used
        lamps to fill the voids.
    French Fries: [lead], satiric piece about a woman whose
        favorite food is a hamburger from MacDonald's.

THIRD AND OAK
    Alberta: [lead], meticulous, quiet, refined, self contained,
        holds pain of her husband's death inside.

THYMUS VULGARIS
    Ruby: [lead], warm, loving, common, depressed, sad, married
        many times.

TOP GIRLS
    Isabella Bird: [supporting role], 19th century individ-
        ualist, independent, traveled around the world extensive-
        ly from age 40 to 70.

A TOUCH OF MARBLE
    Miss Carroll: [short role], brisk school administrator.
    Aunt Margaret: [short role], exacerbated nerves, bitter.

TREVOR
    Mrs. Lawrence: [supporting role], free thinking mother from
        suburbs.
    Mrs. Kempton: [supporting role], conventional middle class
        matron.

TROUBLE IN MIND
    Wiletta: [lead], savy, stage performer, speaks mind, good
        singing voice, [black].

TROUBLE IN MIND
    Wiletta: [lead], savy, stage performer, speaks mind, good
        singing voice, [black].

TWIGS
    Dorothy: [lead], suburban housewife celebrating 25th wed-
        ding anniversary.

TWO O'CLOCK FEEDING
    Dr. Simmons: [short role], pediatrician, supportive,
        professional, [black].

VERONICA'S ROOM
    The woman: [lead], changes identities, mysterious, insane.

A VERY RICH WOMAN
    Edith: [supporting role], pretty, chic, has affectations,
        greedy, dishonest.
    Ursala: [supporting role], chic, artificial, shallow, self-centered

    Grace: [supporting role], feels useless, children have
        grown up.

VICTORY ON MRS. DANDYWINE'S ISLAND
    Mrs. Dandywine: [lead], stout, perfect manners, meticulous
        elocution, superior voice.
    Miss Companion: [lead], thin, refined, hair turning gray,
        impressionable, excitable.
    Miss Liveforever: [short role], red hair, wild makeup, out-
        spoken in the extreme, total lack of manners.

A VOICE OF MY OWN
    flexible casting- each performer can play several roles
        covering famous personalities from women's history.

WAITING FOR THE PARADE
    Margaret: [supporting role], fearful, worried about sons at
        war, pessimistic.

WEST SIDE WALTZ
    Clara: [lead], rotund, bright make-up, jolly, plays violin,
        overprotective.

WOMANSPEAK
    Abigail Adams: [supporting role], writer, scholar, advocate
        of women's rights, lived during American revolution, wife
        of John Adams.
    Sojourner Truth: [supporting role], black slave, eloquent
        spokesperson for civil rights circa 1850.
    Harriet Beecher Stowe: [supporting role], abolitionist,
        highly influential author of Uncle Tom's Cabin which
        exposed the evils of slavery.
    Anna Carroll: [supporting role], researcher, author of
        Tennessee Plan which helped the North to win the Civil
        war.

Susan B. Anthony: [supporting role], organizer of women's
    suffrage campaign.
Victoria Woodhull: [supporting role], advocate for equal
    rights, abortion, and free love, ran for U.S. president.
Mother Jones: [supporting role], courageous organizer of the
    United Mine Workers.
Adelita: [supporting role], soldier in New Mexico in 1913,
    follower of Pancho Villa.
Margaret Sanger: [supporting role], leader of the birth
    control movement in 1917.
Eleanor Roosevelt: [supporting role], advocate for social
    causes, writer, lecturer, wife of Franklin Roosevelt.
Emma Goldman: [supporting role], anarchist, activist.

A YOUNG LADY OF PROPERTY
    Miss Gert: [supporting role], aunt, tall, good looking,
        solid.
    Minna: [supporting role], thin, strong, domestic, maternal,
        [black].

Character Ages 60 and Over

THE AMERICAN DREAM
    Grandma: [lead], feisty, crafty, nasty.

AND MISS REARDON DRINKS A LITTLE
    Mrs. Pentrano: [short role], comic, sells cosmetics, mala-
        prop.

AUGUSTUS
    Duchess: [lead], matriarch, grandmother, imposing, elegant.

AUNTIE MAME
    Mother Burnside: [short role], in wheelchair, formidable.

THE AUTUMN GARDEN
    Mary Ellis: [supporting role], sometimes sprightly, other
        times senile.

A BAD YEAR FOR TOMATOES
    Cora Gump: [supporting role], small town, friendly, well
        meaning, trite.
    Reba Harper: [supporting role], gossip, conventional, pro-
        vincial.
    Willa Mae Wilcox: [supporting role], furtive, interested in
        the occult.

BEAUTY AND THE BEAST
    Mrs. C. Crunch: [lead], witch, gruff, practical, comic.

Madame Suzanne: [supporting role], fairy, French accent, extravagant.

LES BELLES SOEURS
Olivine: [short role], comic, wheelchair, infantile, bites.

BERTHE
Berthe: [lead], garish, wears wildly shaped, glittery blue plastic glasses, worldly, crude, disappointed.

BITS AND PIECES
Mrs. Eberly: [short role], homespun, brusque, religious.

BONJOUR LA BONJOUR
Albertine: [supporting role], aunt, watches TV constantly.
Charlotte: [supporting role], aunt, complains about health, critical, suspicious, vindictive.

THE BRIDAL NIGHT
Mrs. Sullivan: [supporting role], mother of mad man, narrates action and takes part in it.

CATSPLAY
Ersi: [lead], compassionate, agile, nervous.
Giza: [lead], crippled sister.
Paula: [supporting role], friend, determined, tries to hide age.
Mrs. Adelaide Vivelli: [short role], ex-Wagnerian diva, haughty.

THE CHALK GARDEN
Mrs. St. Maugham: [lead], eccentric, overpowering, indulgent towards granddaughter.

THE COCKTAIL PARTY
Julia: [supporting role], worldly socialite, poised, sophisticated.

CROWN MATRIMONIAL
Queen Mary: [lead], stately monarch, proper, traditional.
Lady Arlie [supporting role], lady in waiting, loyal confidant.

THE CURIOUS SAVAGE
Mrs. Savage: [lead], sensible, loving, committed, zestful.

THE DARK OF THE MOON AND THE FULL
Grandma: [lead], sardonic, mischievous, drinks too much.

DENTIST AND PATIENT
Anybody: [lead], naive dentist, honest, gullible chump.
Anybody else: [lead], millionaire, crafty, unscrupulous, stingy.

DESIGN FOR LIVING
    Miss Hodge: [short role], untidy, comic servant.

DUCHESSE DE LANGEAIS
    La Duchesse: [lead], retired prostitute, lively, French, has
    had eventful life, sexually explicit, coarse.

THE EFFECT OF GAMMA RAYS
    Nanny: [short role], senile, non speaking.

EVERYBODY HAS TO BE SOMEBODY
    Maggie: [lead], vivid, energetic, sense of humor, domineer-
    ing.
    Birdie: [supporting role], stage mother, well dressed,
    wealthy, gentle.

THE EYE OF THE BEHOLDER
    Jane: [lead], slim, fair, intellectual, artistic style cool
    and classical.
    Bella: [lead], heavy set, dark, emotional, artistic style
    intense, free, loose, abandoned.
    Leona: [supporting role], model, attractive, opinionated,
    joins in conversation.

FIRST BREEZE OF SUMMER
    Gremmar: [supporting role], religious, conservative, lives
    in past, [black].

FOR THE USE OF THE HALL
    Bess: [supporting role], narrates action, elegant, authori-
    tative.

FORTY CARATS
    Maud Hayes: [supporting role], mother.
    Mrs. Margolin: any age, [short role], secretary.

FUNNYHOUSE OF A NEGRO
    Queen Victoria: [supporting role], has back turned to
    audience, wears white mask.
    Duchess of Hapsburg: [supporting role], has back turned to
    audience, wears white mask.

GERTRUDE STEIN
    Gertrude Stein: [lead], writer, unconventional, individual-
    ist, powerful.

THE GIN GAME
    Fonsia: [lead], timid, lonely, self-righteous, judgmental.

GOING TO SEE THE ELEPHANT
    Maw Wheeler: [lead], energetic, strong willed pioneer woman
    with worn face.

GOLDA
    Golda: [lead], determined, idealistic, formidable Prime
        Minister of Israel.

GOODBYE MY FANCY
    Miss Shakleford: [supporting role], alumnae secretary,
        harsh, proper.

HOT L BALTIMORE
    Milly: [supporting role], has ability to see ghosts, spaced
        out.
    Mrs. Billotti: [supporting role], mother of thief evicted
        from hotel.

IN THE DESERT OF MY SOUL
    Ma: [lead], tough, foul-mouthed, blunt, but caring.

JOE EGG
    Grace: [supporting role], suburban, fastidious, dresses in
        frills.

THE KILLING OF SISTER GEORGE
    Madam Xenia: [supporting role], fortune teller, exotic
        dress, beads.

KILLINGS ON THE LAST LINE
    Betty: [supporting role], factory worker, widow, [black].
    Day Tripper: [short role], part-time maintenance worker,
        [black].

THE LADIES SHOULD BE IN BED
    Old woman: [very short], mother.

THE LAST OF MRS. LINCOLN
    Mrs. McCullough: [supporting role], old friend, talkative,
        trite, shallow.

LET ME HEAR YOU SMILE
    Hannah: [lead], homebody kindergarten teacher.

LET ME HEAR YOU WHISPER
    Helen: [lead], cleaning lady in laboratory, tender hearted.
    Dr. Crocus: [short role], scientist performs weird experi-
        ments.
    Ms. Fridge: [short role], assistant, not very bright,
        obedient.

A LOVELY SUNDAY FOR CREVE COEUR
    Miss Gluck: [short role], humorous, German speaking.

LOVERS
    Mrs. Wilson: [supporting role], invalid domineering, manipu-
        lative.
    Cissy: [supporting role], small and frail.

THE LOVES OF CASS MCGUIRE
    Cass: [lead], tall, gaudily dressed, chain smoker, vulgar.
    Mother: [short role], in wheelchair.
    Mrs. Butcher: [short role], new resident of nursing home.

THE MADWOMAN OF CHAILLOT
    Countess Aurelia: [lead], indomitable optimist, loves life,
        wildly eccentric, clever.
    Mme. Constance: [supporting role], comic, elaborate, dainty,
        large hat.
    Mlle. Gabrielle: [supporting role], outdated dress, overdone
        makeup, coy, has imaginary dog following her.
    Mme. Josephine: [supporting role], fantastically dressed,
        out of touch with reality, majestic.

A MATTER OF GRAVITY
    Mrs. Basil: [lead], gallant, upper class, trying to be
        realistic.

MEMOIR
    Sarah: [lead], grandiose, romantic, enchanting, tempera-
        mental, fiercely independent, has one leg amputated.

THE MIDNIGHT CALLER
    Miss Rowena: [supporting role], coy southern belle, roman-
        tic, teacher.

MORNINGS AT SEVEN
    Esther: [supporting role], cheerful, once a beauty, fun
        loving.
    Cora: [supporting role], easy going, jealous of sister.
    Ida: [supporting role], reluctant to let son go, husband has
        spells.
    Arronetta: [supporting role], independent, loves sister's
        husband.

'NIGHT MOTHER
    Thelma: [lead], conventional, ordinary, recently widowed.

NIGHT THOUGHTS
    Dorothy: [lead], weak, invalid, lonely, difficult, sus-
        picious.
    Ida: [lead], healthy, energetic, tries to encourage Dorothy.

ONCE A CATHOLIC
    Mother Basil: [supporting role], nun, short, fat, nags
        students.

ON GOLDEN POND
    Ethel Thayer: [lead], small, energetic, peacemaker.

OPAL'S BABY
    Granny: [supporting role], tiny, wild-eyed, crazy, hoodlum.

OPAL'S HUSBAND
    Velma [supporting role], daughter, mean, aggressive, large.

OPENING NIGHT
    Fanny Ellis: [lead], clever, star, tough trouper, alcoholic.
    Hecky: [supporting role], maid, companion, dresser.

OUT OF OUR FATHER'S HOUSE
    Elizabeth Cady Stanton: [lead], women's suffrage movement
        founder, mother of large family.
    "Mother" Mary Jones: [lead], organized labor in 19th cent-
        ury.
    Dr. Anna Howard Shaw: [lead], medical doctor and minister.
    Maria Mitchell: [lead], astronomer, hungry for knowledge.
    Elizabeth Gertrude Stern: [lead], career woman and writer
        from the Jewish ghetto.

PIZZA
    Sadie: [supporting role], narrow minded busy-body, friend of
        Lena.
    Lena: [lead], overprotective possessive mother, boisterous,
        generous, superstitious.

PLEASE, NO FLOWERS
    Lena Grosman: [lead], now a ghost, was tired of life.
    Mrs. Bleeker: [short role], fair-weather friend of Lena.
    Mrs. Lehr: [short role], fair-weather friend of Lena.

PORCH
    Dot: [lead], in wheelchair, controlling, clinging to
        daughter.

THE PRIMARY ENGLISH CLASS
    Mrs. Pong: [short role], Chinese-speaking.

A RAISIN IN THE SUN
    Lena Younger: [lead], powerful matriarch, strong authority,
        subtle beauty and grace, white hair, noble carriage,
        [black].

REFLECTIONS IN A WINDOW
    Bertie: [supporting role], small, frail, spirited, alert,
        plucky.
    Alice: [supporting role], Bertie's daughter, quiet,
        friendly, kind, loving.
    Martha: [supporting role], small, quiet, likable, loving
        towards others.
    Ruth: [supporting role], strong willed, tries to walk
        despite crippling arthritis.
    Esther: [supporting role], wheelchair, lots of jewelry,
        raspy voice.
    Rebecca: [supporting role], enormous body, can't walk, in
        wheelchair.
    Margaret: [short role], sad, unhappy, in wheelchair.

THE RIMERS OF ELDRITCH
Mary Windrod: [supporting role], senile, lost in memories, paranoid.

ROOM FOR ONE WOMAN
Pedley: [lead], uses two canes to walk, afraid, reminisces.
Besley: [lead], new tenant, cheerful, robust, anger underneath.

SAVE ME A PLACE AT FOREST LAWN
Clara: [lead], bossy, assertive, self satisfied, knows it all.
Gertrude: [lead], fearful, emotional, but spunky, realistic.

SECOND CHANCE
Rita: [lead], energetic, life-loving, planning to perform in play wearing leotard and tights.
Evelyn: [lead], conservative, tries to get friend to slow down.

THE SECRET AFFAIRS OF MILDRED WILD
Helen: [supporting role], angry sister-in-law.

SEPARATE CEREMONIES
Grace: [supporting role], aunt, nurturing, likes to cook, traditional.

SKIRMISHES
Mother: [supporting role], on her deathbed, paralyzed stroke victim, unable to talk.

SOMETHING UNSPOKEN
Miss Cornelia Scott: [lead], grandly pretentious, aristocratic.

STANDARD SAFETY
Mrs. MacIntosh: [short role], personnel director, mean, petty.

STEAMING
Mrs. Meadow: [supporting role], prissy, overprotective, bossy.

STOOP
Second woman: [lead], thin, resigned.

TALKING WITH...
Lamps: [lead], a woman in later years describes how she used lamps to fill the voids.
French Fries: [lead], satiric piece about a woman whose favorite food is a hamburger from MacDonald's.

TENNESSEE
Old Woman: [lead], strong willed, eccentric.
Neighbor: [short role], friend of old woman.

THIRD AND OAK
    Alberta: [lead], meticulous, quiet, refined, hides pain.

THYMUS VULGARIS
    Ruby: [lead], warm, loving, common, depressed, often mar-
        ried.

TOP GIRLS
    Isabella Bird: [supporting role], 19th century individ-
        ualist, traveled extensively from 40 to 70 years of age.

TWIGS
    Ma: [lead], failing but tough, Irish.

UNCOMMON WOMEN
    Mrs. Plumm: [supporting role], prim house mother.

VERONICA'S ROOM
    The woman: [lead], changes identities, mysterious, insane.

A VERY RICH WOMAN
    Mrs. Lord: [lead], vital, chic, snappy dresser, wears make-
        up.
    Mrs. Minot: [supporting role], proper Bostonian, con-
        servative dresser.

A VOICE OF MY OWN
    flexible casting- one performer can play several roles
        covering famous personalities from women's history.

VOICES
    Kate: [supporting role], performer who choose career over
        family.

WEST SIDE WALTZ
    Margaret Mary: [lead], staunch, proud, peppery, sense of
        humor, emotionally distant, plays piano.

WINGS
    Emily Stilson: [lead], stroke victim, frightened, frus-
        trated.
    Mrs. Timmins: [short role], stroke victim.

WOMANSPEAK
    Contemporary Woman: [lead], central figure who con-
        verses with women from the past.
    Abigail Adams: [supporting role], writer, scholar, advocate
        of women's rights, lived during American revolution, wife
        of John Adams.
    Sojourner Truth: [supporting role], black slave, eloquent
        spokesperson for civil rights circa 1850.
    Harriet Beecher Stowe: [supporting role], abolitionist,
        highly influential author of Uncle Tom's Cabin which
        exposed the evils of slavery.

Anna Carroll: [supporting role], researcher, author of the
    Tennessee Plan which helped the North to win the Civil
    war.
Susan B. Anthony: [supporting role], organizer of women's
    suffrage campaign.
Victoria Woodhull: [supporting role], advocate for equal
    rights, abortion, and free love, ran for U.S. president.
Mother Jones: [supporting role], courageous organizer of the
    United Mine Workers.
Adelita: [supporting role], soldier in New Mexico in 1913,
    follower of Pancho Villa.
Margaret Sanger: [supporting role], leader of the birth
    control movement in 1917.
Eleanor Roosevelt: [supporting role], advocate for social
    causes, writer, lecturer, wife of Franklin Roosevelt.
Emma Goldman: [supporting role], anarchist, activist.

Character Types

Although contemporary theater doesn't employ stock character types as was done in the past, many roles tend to fall into rough categories. The listing below represents an attempt at such a classification. Not every role will have all the characteristics mentioned, there will be overlapping, and one character may fit into more than one category; but this scheme will aid the performer looking for a particular kind of role to play.

Heroic
Brave, outspoken, champion of causes, breaking out of the mold, asserting individuality.

Kind and Nurturing
Warm, maternal, loving, kind, supportive, sympathetic, humanistic.

Comic
Humorous, satirical, silly, clown, witty.

Villainous
Mean, evil, wicked, nasty, violent, oppressive, destructive.

Tragic
Victim of life, pathetic, hard luck, beset with woe, miserable, trapped by circumstances.

Unique
Unusual, exotic, one of a kind, extraordinary, singular.

High Brow
Wealthy, well off, sophisticated, cultured royalty.

Low Brow
Impoverished, oppressed, down and out, common, lowly prostitute.

Disturbed
Compulsive, neurotic, psychotic, delusional, violent, spaced out, criminal, insane.

Heroic

AGNES OF GOD
    Dr. Martha Livingstone
    Mother Miriam Ruth

AM I BLUE?
    Ashbe

AN ALMOST PERFECT PERSON
    Irene Porter

AUNTIE MAME
    Auntie Mame

BELLE OF AMHERST
    Emily Dickinson

BITS AND PIECES
    Iris

BLACK GIRL
    Billie Jean

CANADIAN GOTHIC
    Jean

CATSPLAY
    Ersi

THE CHALK GARDEN
    Madrigal

CHARACTER LINES
    Linda

CHILDREN OF A LESSER GOD
    Sarah

A CLEARING IN THE WOODS
    Virginia

CLOTHES FOR A SUMMER HOTEL
    Zelda

CONFESSIONS OF A FEMALE
    DISORDER
    Ronnie

THE CORRUPTERS
    Rachel Crane

CRIMES OF THE HEART
    Babe

CROWN MATRIMONIAL
    Queen Mary

THE CURIOUS SAVAGE
    Mrs. Savage

EDUCATING RITA
    Rita

THE EFFECTS OF GAMMA RAYS
    Tillie

FAVOURITE NIGHTS
    Catherine

THE FIRST MONDAY IN OCTOBER
    Ruth Loomis

FOR COLORED GIRLS
    Dancers

THE FROGS
    Masie

GERTRUDE STEIN
    Gertrude Stein

GETTING OUT
    Arlene

GIFT OF MURDER!
    Stella

GOING TO SEE THE ELEPHANT
    Ma Wheeler
    Sara Wheeler
    Etta Bailey
    Helene Nichols

GOLDA
    Golda

GOODBYE MY FANCY
    Agatha Reed
    Grace Woods

HAY FEVER
    Judith Bliss

I JUST WANTED SOMEONE TO KNOW
    many figures from labor
        history

THE INDEPENDENT FEMALE
    Sarah Bullit

JESSIE AND THE BANDIT QUEEN
    Belle Starr

JOSEPHINE: THE MOUSE SINGER
    Josephine

THE KILLING OF SISTER GEORGE
    June

KILLINGS ON THE LAST LINE
    Starkey

LADIES AT THE ALAMO
    Dede Cooper

THE LARK
    Joan

LET ME HEAR YOU WHISPER
    Helen

LETTERS HOME
    Sylvia Plath

LOOSE ENDS
    Susan

THE LOVES OF CASS MCGUIRE
    Cass

THE MADWOMAN OF CHAILLOT
    Countess Aurelia

MAJOR BARBARA
    Barbara Undershaft

A MATTER OF GRAVITY
    Mrs. Basil

MAUD GONNE SAYS NO TO THE POET
    Maud

MEMOIR
    Sarah Bernhardt

THE MIDNIGHT CALLER
    Helen

THE MIRACLE WORKER
    Annie Sullivan
    Helen Keller

A MOON FOR THE MISBEGOTTEN
    Josie

MRS. DALLY HAS A LOVER
    Evalyn

NUTS
    Claudia

OPENING NIGHT
    Fanny

OUT OF OUR FATHER'S HOUSE
    Elizabeth Cady Stanton
    "Mother" Mary Jones
    Dr. Anna Howard Shaw
    Maria Mitchell
    Elizabeth Gertrude Stern

THE PRIME OF MISS JEAN BRODIE
    Jean Brodie

A RAISIN IN THE SUN
    Lena Younger
    Beneatha Younger

REFLECTIONS IN A WINDOW
    Bertie
    Ruth

THE RIMERS OF ELDRITCH
    Eva

SAFE HOUSE
    Hillary

THE SEA HORSE
  Gertrude

SECOND CHANCE
  Rita

6 RMS RIV VU
  Janet

SLAM THE DOOR SOFTLY
  Nora

STUFFINGS
  Gladys Koontz

SUNSET/SUNRISE
  Gem
  Dianne

TODAY IS INDEPENDENCE DAY
  Evalyn

TOP GIRLS
  Marlene
  Isabella Bird
  Lady Nijo
  Pope Joan

THE TWELVE POUND LOOK
  Kate

TWO SIDES OF DARKNESS
  Melena
  Jenny
  chorus

UNCOMMON WOMEN
  Kate Quinn

UP THE DOWN STAIRCASE
  Sylvia Barrett

VIVAT! REGINIA!
  Mary
  Elizabeth

A VOICE OF MY OWN
  Women

VOICES
  Maya
  Kate

WAITING FOR THE PARADE
  Catherine

WEST SIDE WALTZ
  Margaret Mary

WAITING FOR THE PARADE
  Catherine

WINE IN THE WILDERNESS
  Tommy

WINGS
  Emily Stilson

WOMANSPEAK
  Abigail Adams
  Sojourner Truth
  Harriet Beecher Stowe
  Anna Carroll
  Susan B. Anthony
  Victoria Woodhull
  Mother Jones
  Adelita
  Margaret Sanger
  Eleanor Roosevelt
  Emma Goldman

A YOUNG LADY OF PROPERTY
  Wilma Thompson

Kind and Nurturing

AND IF THAT MOCKING BIRD
  DON'T SING
    Casey
    Darlene

BEAUTY AND THE BEAST
    Mrs. C. Crunch
    Beauty

BITS AND PIECES
    Helen

THE BRIDAL NIGHT
    Mrs. Sullivan
    Miss Regan

BUTTERFLIES ARE FREE
    Mrs. Baker

CASTLE IN THE VILLAGE
    Lydia

CHAPTER TWO
    Jennie Malone
    Faye Medwick

CHILDREN OF A LESSER GOD
    Lydia

CRIMES OF THE HEART
    Lenny

THE CURIOUS SAVAGE
    Whilhelmina

DARK OF THE MOON AND THE
  FULL
    Helen

FINISHING TOUCHES
    Katy

FIRST BREEZE OF SUMMER
    Aunt Edna

FOR THE USE OF THE HALL
    Alice

FORTY CARATS
    Ann Stanley
    Maud Hayes

THE FROGS
    Mrs. Tupper
    Miss Phillips

GETTING OUT
    Ruby

I OUGHT TO BE IN PICTURES
    Steffy

JACOB'S LADDER
    Leona
    Annie

JOE EGG
    Sheila
    Grace

THE LADY FROM DUBUQUE
    Elizabeth

LADYHOUSE BLUES
    Liz

LET ME HEAR YOU SMILE
    Hannah

LETTERS HOME
    Aurellia

LOOK: WE'VE COME THROUGH
    Belle Dort

LOOSE ENDS
    Maraya
    Selina

A LOVELY SUNDAY FOR CREVE
  COUER
    Bodey

A MEMBER OF THE WEDDING
    Berenice

THE MIDNIGHT CALLER
    Helen
    Mrs. Crawford

MIMOSA PUDICA
    Dianne

MORNINGS AT SEVEN
    Esther
    Cora
    Myrtle

ON GOLDEN POND
    Ethel Thayer

OPENING NIGHT
    Hecky

ROADS TO HOME
    Mabel
    Vonnie

ROOMFUL OF ROSES
    Nancy
    Grace

SAFE HOUSE
    Ruth

SAME TIME NEXT YEAR
    Doris

THE SAND CASTLE
    Irene

SEPARATE CEREMONIES
    Carrie
    Grace

6 RMS RIV VU
    Anne

STANDARD SAFETY
    Denise
    Andrea

STRING
    Mrs. Beverly
    Maydelle

SUNSET/SUNRISE
    Louise

TALKING WITH...
    Clear Glass Marbles
    Lamps
    Dragons

TALLEY'S FOLLY
    Sally

TENNESSEE
    Mary

THIRD AND OAK
    Deedee

THYMUS VULGARIS
    Evelyn

TREVOR
    Mrs. Kempton

TROUBLE IN MIND
    Willetta
    Judy

TWO O'CLOCK FEEDING
    Louise
    Marie
    Dr. Simmons

UNCOMMON WOMEN
    Samantha
    Muffet
    Holly

UP THE DOWN STAIRCASE
    Sylvia
    Beatrice
    Ellen

VERONICA'S ROOM
    Susan

A VERY RICH WOMAN
    Mrs. Minot
    Daphne

VIVAT! REGINA!
    Queen Mary

VOICES
    Rosalinde
    Grace

WAITING FOR THE PARADE
    Catherine
    Margaret

WINGS
    Amy

A YOUNG LADY OF PROPERTY
    Arabella
    Miss Gert
    Minna
    Mrs. Leighton

Comic

AUNTIE MAME
    Vera
    Agnes Gooch

THE AUTOGRAPH HOUND
    Lila
    Cissie

BEAUTY AND THE BEAST
    Mrs. C. Crunch
    Madame Suzanne
    Hyacinth
    Petunia

BEDROOM FARCE
    Kate
    Susannah

BELL BOOK AND CANDLE
    Miss Holroyd

LES BELLES SOEURS
    Germaine
    Gabrielle
    Olivine
    Lisette

BLIND DATE
    Angie

BRINGING IT ALL BACK HOME
    Mother
    Daughter
    Miss Horne

BUTTERFLIES ARE FREE
    Jill

CALIFORNIA SUITE
    Beth
    Gert

CALM DOWN MOTHER
    Women

CASTLE IN THE VILLAGE
    Mrs. Goldfine

A COUPLA WHITE CHICKS
    Maude
    Hannah

DESIGN FOR LIVING
    Gilda
    Miss Hodge

FINISHING TOUCHES
    Katy

A GOOD TIME
    Mandy Morgan

HAY FEVER
    Judith Bliss
    Myra Arundel

THE INDEPENDENT FEMALE
    Sarah Bullit
    Gloria Pennybank
    Matilda Pennybank

THE KNIGHT AT THE TWELFTH
    SAUCER
    Rose
    Shanakind

THE LAST OF THE RED HOT LOVERS
    Elaine
    Bobbi
    JEANETTE

LEMONADE
    Mabel
    Edith

LET ME HEAR YOU WHISPER
    Dr. Crocus
    Ms. Fridge

LUNCH HOUR
    Carrie

THE MADWOMAN OF CHAILLOT
    Aurelia
    Constance
    Gabrielle

OPAL SERIES
    Opal
    Rosie

A PHOENIX TOO FREQUENT
    Dynamene
    Doto

Comic (con't)

PLEASE, NO FLOWERS
    Lena
    Esther

PRIMARY ENGLISH CLASS
    Debbie Westba

SEASCAPE
    Sarah

SECRET AFFAIRS OF MILDRED WILD
    Mildred
    Berthe

SISTER MARY IGNATIUS
    Sister Mary Ignatius
    Diane
    Philomena

SURPRISE, SURPRISE
    Jeannine
    Laurette
    Madeleine

THIS BIRD OF DAWNING
    Nancy

TREVOR
    Sarah
    Jane
    Mrs. Lawrence

VICTORY ON MRS. DANDYWINE'S
  ISLAND
    Mrs. Dandywine
    Miss Companion
    Miss Liveforever

Villainous

AND
    Ruth

THE AMERICAN DREAM
    Mommy
    Grandma

COME INTO THE GARDEN, MAUD
    Anna-Mary

THE CORRUPTERS
    Boots
    Liz
    Frankie

CRIMES OF THE HEART
    Chick

THE CURIOUS SAVAGE
    Lily Belle

DENTIST AND PATIENT
    Anybody Else

THE DRAPES COME
    Mrs. Fiers
    Barbara

THE FLOUNDER COMPLEX
    Woman

GETTING OUT
    Mother

THE KILLING OF SISTER GEORGE
    June

LADIES AT THE ALAMO
    Bella

THE LADIES SHOULD BE IN BED
    Maggie
    Charlotte

LET ME HEAR YOU WHISPER
    Miss Moray
    Dr. Crocus
    Ms. Fridge

LOVERS
    Mrs. Wilson

Villainous (con't)
LOVERS
    Mrs. Wilson

THE MAIDS
    Solange
    Clair

MISS MARGARIDA'S WAY
    Miss Margarida

MY SISTER IN THIS HOUSE
    Madame Danzard

OH DAD, POOR DAD
    Madame Rosepettle

EVERYBODY LOVES OPAL
    Gloria

OPAL'S BABY
    Verna
    Granny

OPAL'S HUSBAND
    Velma

OPAL'S MILLION DOLLAR DUCK
    Queenie

PORCH
    Dot

THE PRIME OF MISS JEAN BRODIE
    Miss MacKay

THE RIMERS OF ELDRITCH
    Evelyn
    Nelly
    Mary
    Martha
    Wilma

SHOUT ACROSS RIVER
    Christine

SOMETHING UNSPOKEN
    Miss Cornelia Scott

STANDARD SAFETY
    Mary Farrell
    Mrs. MacIntosh

Tragic

AGNES OF GOD
    Agnes

THE BELLE OF AMHERST
    Emily

LES BELLES SOEURS
    Marie-Ange
    Des Neiges

BERTHE
    Berthe

BOSEMAN AND LENA
    Lena

THE BRIDAL NIGHT
    Mrs. Sullivan

THE CORRUPTERS
    Carol Ramirez

DUSA, FISH, STAS, AND VI
    Dusa
    Fish
    Stas
    Vi

THE EFFECTS OF GAMMA RAYS
    Beatrice

THE FLOUNDER COMPLEX
    Girl

FOR COLORED GIRLS
    Dancers

GETTING OUT
    Arlene

I LOST A PAIR OF GLOVES
    YESTERDAY
    Actress

KILLINGS ON THE LAST LINE
    Ellis

THE LADY FROM DUBUQUE
    Jo

LADY OF LARKSPUR LOTION
    Mrs. Hardwicke-Moore

THE LAST OF MRS. LINCOLN
   Mary Todd Lincoln

LETTERS HOME
   Sylvia

LOOK AWAY
   Mary Todd Lincoln

LOVERS
   Mag
   Hannah

THE LOVES OF CASS MCGUIRE
   Cass

THE MAIDS
   Madame

MOJO
   Irene

MY SISTER IN THIS HOUSE
   Christine
   Lea
   Isabelle Danzard

NEVIS MT. DEW
   Zepora
   Everelda
   Billie

'NIGHT MOTHER
   Thelma
   Jessie

NIGHT THOUGHTS
   Dorothy

NUTS
   Claudia

A PALM TREE IN A ROSE GARDEN
   Barbara

PORCH
   Lucille

A RAISIN IN THE SUN
   Ruth

REFLECTIONS IN A WINDOW
   Rebecca
   Margaret

ROADS TO HOME
   Annie

ROOM FOR ONE WOMAN
   Pedley

SNOWANGEL
   Connie

STAGE DIRECTIONS
   Ruth
   Ruby

STOOP
   First Woman
   Second Woman
   Third Woman

THIRD AND OAK
   Alberta

VERONICA'S ROOM
   Susan

VOICES
   Erin

Unique

THE AMERICAN DREAM
    Grandma

AUTOGRAPH HOUND
    Lila

BAD YEAR FOR TOMATOES
    Wila Mae

BAG LADY
    Clara

BEAUTY AND THE BEAST
    Mrs. C. Crunch
    Madame Suzanne

THE BICYCLE RIDERS
    Patsy

CRAB DANCE
    Sadie Golden

DARK OF THE MOON AND THE FULL
    Grandma

THE DARNING NEEDLE
    Betty
    Ida

LA DUCHESS DE LANGAIS
    La Duchesse

DUSA, FISH, STAS, AND VI
    Stas

GERTRUDE STEIN
    Gertrude Stein

IN THE DESSERT OF MY SOUL
    Ma

JESSIE AND THE BANDIT QUEEN
    Belle Starr

THE KILLING OF SISTER GEORGE
    Madam Xenia

THE MADWOMAN OF CHAILLOT
    Constance
    Aurelia
    Gabrielle

MAUD GONNE SAYS NO TO THE POET
    Maud

MEMOIR
    Sarah Bernhardt

MISS MARGARIDA'S WAY
    Miss Margarida

OH DAD, POOR DAD
    Madame Rosepettle

OUT OF OUR FATHER'S HOUSE
    Elizabeth Cady Stanton
    Maria Mitchell
    "Mother" Mary Jones
    Dr. Anna Howard Shaw

A PALM TREE IN A ROSE GARDEN
    Rose Frobisher

PIZZA
    Perla

REFLECTIONS IN A WINDOW
    Bertie

SAFE HOUSE
    Hillary
    Tink

SEASCAPE
    Sarah

THE SEA HORSE
    Gertrude

THE SECRET AFFAIRS OF MILDRED
WILD
    Mildred

SISTER MARY IGNATIUS EXPLAINS
IT ALL
    Sister Mary Ignatius

STUFFINGS
    Gladys Koontz

TALKING WITH...
    Scraps
    Rodeo
    Twirler

Unique (con't)
TALKING WITH...(con't)
    Handler
    French Fries
    Marks

TOP GIRLS
    Isabella Bird
    Lady Nijo
    Dull Gret
    Pope Joan
    Patient Griselda

VERONICA'S ROOM
    The Woman

A VERY RICH WOMAN
    Mrs. Lord

VICTORY ON MRS. DANDYWINE'S
  ISLAND
    Mrs. Liveforever

WOMANSPEAK
    Abigail Adams
    Sojourner Truth
    Harriet Beecher Stowe
    Anna Carroll
    Susan B. Anthony
    Victoria Woodhull
    Mother Jones
    Adelita
    Margaret Sanger
    Eleanor Roosevelt
    Emma Goldman

High Brow

AUGUSTUS
    Duchess

AUNTIE MAME
    Auntie Mame
    Vera
    Doris Upson
    Gloria Upson

THE AU PAIR MAN
    Mrs. Rogers

THE CHALK GARDEN
    Mrs. St. Maughm
    Laurel
    Olivia

THE CHINESE RESTAURANT
  SYNDROME
    Susan
    Maggie

COME INTO THE GARDEN, MAUD
    Maud

THE COCKTAIL PARTY
    Julia
    Celia
    Lavinia

CROWN MATRIMONIAL
    Queen Mary
    Mary
    Alice
    Elizabeth

DESIGN FOR LIVING
    Gilda
    Helen
    Grace

FALLEN ANGELS
    Jane
    Julia

FAVOURITE NIGHTS
    Catherine

FIRST MONDAY IN OCTOBER
    Ruth Loomis

High Brow (con't)

GOLDA
    Golda

GOODBYE MY FANCY
    Agatha Reed
    Miss Shakleford

HAY FEVER
    Judith
    Sorel
    Myra

I AM A CAMERA
    Mrs. Watson-Courtneidge

THE LARK
    Little Queen
    Agnes Sorel
    Queen Yolande

THE MADWOMAN OF CHAILLOT
    Countess Aurelia
    Mme. Constance
    Mlle. Gabrielle
    Mme. Josephine

MAJOR BARBARA
    Lady Britomart
    Sarah

A MATTER OF GRAVITY
    Mrs. Basil

MEMOIR
    Sarah Bernhardt

MY COUSIN RACHEL
    Louise

THE TWELVE POUND LOOK
    Lady Sims

UNCOMMON WOMEN
    Kate
    Holly
    Susie Friend
    Mrs. Plumm

THE UNDERSTANDING
    Eva
    Acton
    Lydia

A VERY RICH WOMAN
    Mrs. Lord
    Mrs. Minot
    Edith
    Ursala
    Daphne

VICTORY ON MRS. DANDYWINE'S
    ISLAND
        Mrs. Dandywine
        Miss Companion

VIVAT! REGINA!
    Queen Elizabeth
    Queen Mary

WEST SIDE WALTZ
    Margaret Mary

WOMANSPEAK
    Abigail Adams
    Harriet Beecher Stowe
    Eleanor Roosevelt

Low Brow

AM I BLUE?
    Ashbe

AND
    Ruth

AND IF THAT MOCKING BIRD
    DON'T SING
    Casey
    Darlene

BAG LADY
    Clara

BERTHE
    Berthe

BLACK GIRL
    Norma
    Ruth Ann

BLOOD PHOTO
    Angela
    Connie

BOSEMAN AND LENA
    Lena

CHOCOLATE CAKE
    Delia
    Joellen

CLARA'S OLE MAN
    Big Girl
    Clara

THE COAL DIAMOND
    Inez
    Lena
    Betty Jean
    Pearl

COMPANIONS OF THE FIRE
    Woman

THE CORRUPTERS
    Carol
    Boots
    Liz
    Mary
    Frankie

THE DARK OF THE MOON AND THE
    FULL
    Grandma
    Helen

LA DUCHESSE DE LANGAIS
    La Duchesse

DUSA, FISH, STAS, AND VI
    Stas
    Vi

EDUCATING RITA
    Rita

THE EFFECT OF GAMMA RAYS
    Beatrice
    Ruth
    Tillie

FAVOURITE NIGHTS
    Girl

FOR COLORED GIRLS
    Dancers

GETTING OUT
    Arlene
    Arlie
    Ruby
    Mother

HOT L BALTIMORE
    Millie
    Mrs. Bilotti
    April
    Jackie
    Suzy
    Girl

I AM A CAMERA
    Sally

I JUST WANTED SOMEONE TO KNOW
    Labor History Figures

IN THE DESSERT OF MY SOUL
    Ma
    Josie

KILLINGS ON THE LAST LINE
    Starkey
    Hildeman
    Ellis

LADY OF LARKSPUR LOTION
    Mrs. Hardwicke-Moore

THE LOVES OF CASS MCGUIRE
    Cass

LUANN HAMPTON
    LuAnn
    Charmaine
    Claudine

LUDLOW FAIR
    Rachel
    Agnes

THE MAIDS
    Solange
    Claire

MOJO
    Irene

A MOON FOR THE MISBEGOTTEN
    Josie

MY SISTER IN THIS HOUSE
    Christine
    Lea

NUTS
    Claudia

OPAL SERIES
    Opal
    Rosie
    Gloria
    Verna
    Granny
    Queenie

A PERFECT ANALYSIS
    Bessie
    Flora

PIZZA
    Grace
    Lena
    Sadie
    Perla
    Bonsey

PORCH
    Dot
    Lucille

A RAISIN IN THE SUN
    Lena
    Ruth

THE RATTLE OF A SIMPLE MAN
    Cyrenne

REFLECTIONS IN A WINDOW
    Ruth
    Esther
    Rebecca
    Margaret

ROOM FOR ONE WOMAN
    Pedley
    Besley

THE SEA HORSE
    Gertrude

SHOUT ACROSS THE RIVER
    Mrs. Forsythe
    Christine

SISTER MARY IGNATIUS EXPLAINS
  IT ALL FOR YOU
    Diane
    Philomena

SNOWANGEL
    Connie

STEAMING
    Violet

STOOP
    First Woman
    Second Woman
    Third Woman

TENNESSEE
    Old Woman
    Mary

THIRD AND OAK
    Alberta
    Deedee

THYMUS VULGARIS
    Ruby
    Evelyn

TWIGS
    Celia
    Ma

Low Brow (con't)
WEST SIDE WALTZ
    Robin

WINE IN THE WILDERNESS
    Tommy

WOMANSPEAK
    Sojourner Truth

Disturbed

AGNES OF GOD
    Agnes

THE AMERICAN DREAM
    Mommy
    Grandma

AND
    Ruth

AND MISS REARDON DRINKS A
    LITTLE
    Anna

THE BATHTUB
    Joyce

BONJOUR LA BONJOUR
    Albertine
    Charlotte
    Denise
    Monique

BRINGING IT ALL BACK HOME
    Mother
    Daughter

CHOCOLATE CAKE
    Delia
    Joellen

CLOTHES FOR A SUMMER HOTEL
    Zelda

THE CURIOUS SAVAGE
    Fairy Mae
    Florence
    Mrs. Paddy

THE DARK OF THE MOON AND THE
    FULL
    Grandma

A DELICATE BALANCE
    Agnes
    Claire
    Edna
    Julia

THE DRAPES COME
    Mrs. Fiers
    Barbara

DUSA, FISH, STAS, AND VI
    Fish

THE FLOUNDER COMPLEX
    Woman

FUNNYHOUSE OF A NEGRO
    Sarah

GETTING OUT
    Arlie
    Mother

THE GINGERBREAD LADY
    Evy

THE HORSE LATITUDES
    Neva

HOW THE OTHER HALF LOVES
    Mary

KILLINGS ON THE LAST LINE
    Mrs. Starkey

THE KNIGHT AT THE TWELFTH
    SAUCER
    Shanakind

LADY OF LARKSPUR LOTION
    Mrs. Hardwicke-Moore

THE LARK
    Joan

THE LAST OF THE RED HOT LOVERS
    Elaine
    Bobbi
    Jeanette

<u>Disturbed</u> (con't)
LETTERS HOME
      Sylvia

THE MAIDS
      Solange
      Claire

A MATTER OF GRAVITY
      DuBois

MISS MARGARIDA'S WAY
      Miss Margarida

MR. BIGGS
      Eloise
      Mary

MY SISTER IN THIS HOUSE
      Christine
      Lea
      Madame Danzard

'NIGHT MOTHER
      Thelma
      Jessie

NIGHT THOUGHTS
      Dorothy

NUTS
      Claudia

OH DAD, POOR DAD
      Madame Rosepettle

OPENING NIGHT
      Fanny

PATIO
      Pearl

PORCH
      Dot

THE RIMERS OF ELDRITCH
      Mary Windrod

SHOUT ACROSS THE RIVER
      Mrs. Forsythe
      Christine

STEAMING
      Mrs. Meadow
      Dawn

A TOUCH OF MARBLE
      Helen

VERONICA'S ROOM
      Woman

VOICES
      Erin

WINGS
      Emily Stilson

Unusual Physical Characteristics

Overweight

THE AUTOGRAPH HOUND
    Lila

BLACK GIRL
    Norma

BLOOD PHOTO
    Angela

BONJOUR LA BONJOUR
    Denise

CHOCOLATE CAKE
    Delia
    Joellen

CLARA'S OLE MAN
    Big Girl

A CLEARING IN THE WOODS
    Hazelmae

COMPANIONS OF THE FIRE
    Woman

CRIMES OF THE HEART
    Lenny

CROWN MATRIMONIAL
    Duchess of York

THE CURIOUS SAVAGE
    Mrs. Paddy

DARK OF THE MOON AND THE FULL
    Helen

THE EYE OF THE BEHOLDER
    Bella

THE FROGS
    Mrs. Tupper

GERTRUDE STEIN
    Gertrude Stein

GOODBYE MY FANCY
    Ellen Griswold

THE GREAT NEBULA IN ORION
    Carrie

I AM A CAMERA
    Fraulein

THE KILLING OF SISTER GEORGE
    June

THE KNIGHT AT THE TWELFTH
SAUCER
    Rose
    Shanakind

THE LADIES SHOULD BE IN BED
    Charlotte

THE LADY OF LARKSPUR LOTION
    Mrs. Wire

Overweight (con't)
LUANN HAMPTON
    Claudine

A MEMBER OF THE WEDDING
    Berenice Sadie Brown

ONCE A CATHOLIC
    Mother Peter
    Mother Basil
    Mary O'Hennessy

A PALM TREE IN A ROSE GARDEN
    Rose Frobisher
    Mona

PLEASE, NO FLOWERS
    Mrs. Hirshman

SARAH AND THE SAX
    Sarah

STOOP
    First Woman

TWO O'CLOCK FEEDING
    Louise

VICTORY ON MRS. DANDYWINE'S
   ISLAND
    Mrs. Dandywine

WEST SIDE WALTZ
    Clara

Oversize

A MOON FOR THE MISBEGOTTEN
    Josie

THE SEA HORSE
    Gertrude

Wheelchair Bound

AUNTIE MAME
    Mother Burnside

LES BELLES SOEURS
    Olivine

CATSPLAY
    Giza

THE LOVES OF CASS MCGUIRE
    Mother

LUANN HAMPTON
    Claudine

PORCH
    Dot

REFLECTIONS IN A WINDOW
    Esther
    Rebecca
    Margaret

Visual/Hearing Impairments

AUGUSTUS
    Helene (hard of hearing)

CHILDREN OF A LESSER GOD
    Sarah (deaf)
    Lydia (hearing impaired0

THE FLOUNDER COMPLEX
    Woman (nearly blind)

A LOVELY SUNDAY FOR CREVE
   COEUR
    Bodey (hard of hearing)

THE MIRACLE WORKER
    Annie Sullivan (visually
      impaired)
    Helen Keller (deaf and
      blind)

Roles for Minorities

The following plays have roles written for specific minorities. Minority casting is feasible in a wide range of other plays as well.

Asian Women

Loose Ends
Primary English Class

Black Women

And If That Mockingbird Don't Sing
Black Girl
Boseman and Lena
Bringing It All Back Home
Clara's Ole Man
Companions of the Fire
First Breeze of Summer
For Colored Girls Who Have Considered Suicide
Funnyhouse of a Negro
I Just Wanted Someone to Know
Killings on the Last Line
Last of Mrs. Lincoln
Look Away
Member of the Wedding
Miracle Worker
Mojo
Nevis Mountain Dew
Raisin in the Sun
String
This Bird of Dawning
Trouble in Mind
Two O'clock Feeding
Wine in the Wilderness

Hispanic Women

The Corrupters
I Just Wanted Someone to Know
Pizza
Womanspeak

APPENDIX 1:

Plays Classified by Gender Distribution

All Female Casts

One Woman

And
Bag Lady
Belle of Amherst
Berthe
Blank Pages
La Duchesse De Langais
Gertrude Stein
I Lost a Pair of Gloves
   Yesterday
Miss Margarida's Way

Two Women

The Bathtub
Chocolate Cake
A Coupla White Chicks
Dentist and Patient
The Drapes Come
Flounder Complex
The Great Nebula in Orion
Lemonade
Letters Home
Look Away
Ludlow Fair
'Night Mother
Night Thoughts
Opening Night
Patio
Porch
Rouge Atomique
Save Me a Place at Forest Lawn
Second Chance
Something Unspoken
This Bird of Dawning

Three Women

Agnes of God
Calm Down Mother
The Eye of the Beholder
The Frogs
Later
The Maids
Out of Our Father's House
Room for One Woman
Skirmishes
Stoop
Surprise, Surprise

Four Women

The Coal Diamond
Dusa, Fish, Stas, and Vi
The Killing of Sister George
A Lovely Sunday for Creve Coeur
My Sister in This House

Five or More Women

Les Belles Soeurs
The Effect of Gamma Rays
Fefu and Her Friends
For Colored Girls
Ladies at the Alamo
The Ladies Should Be in Bed
Ladyhouse Blues
A Late Snow
Let Me Hear You Whisper
Lunch or Something
Pizza
Steaming

Five Women (con't)

Talking With...
Top Girls
Uncommon Women
A Voice of My Own
Voices
Waiting for the Parade
Womanspeak

PLAYS WITH MIXED CASTS

One Woman

The Bicycle Riders
Blind Date
Boseman and Lena
Companions of the Fire
Crab Dance
Educating Rita
The Gin Game
A Good Time
Jessie and the Bandit Queen
Memoir
Mimosa Pudica
Mojo
A Moon for the Misbegotten
Mrs. Dally Has a Lover
The Rattle of a Simple Man
Same Time Next Year
Sarah and the Sax
The Sea Horse
Slam the Door Softly
Snowangel
Stuffings
Talley's Folly
Today is Independence Day
The Woods

Two Women

And If That Mockingbird Don't
  Sing
Augustus
The Autograph Hound
Bell, Book, and Candle

Two Women (con't)

The Bridal Night
Brontosaurus
Butterflies Are Free
California Suite
Canadian Gothic
Chapter Two
Character Lines
The Chinese Restaurant
  Syndrome
Come Into the Garden, Maud
The Darning Needle
Everybody Loves Opal
First Monday in October
Impromptu
In the Dessert of My Soul
I Ought to Be in Pictures
Jacob's Ladder
Look: We've Come Through
Lunch Hour
Maud Gonne Says No to the Poet
Mr. Biggs
My Cousin Rachel
Oh Dad, Poor Dad
Old Times
On Golden Pond
A Perfect Analysis
A Phoenix Too Frequent
Seascape
Shout Across the River
Stage Directions
Thymus Vulgaris
The Twelve Pound Look
Veronica's Room
Wine in the Wilderness

Three Women

Absent Friends
Absurd Person Singular
The American Dream
Bits and Pieces
Blood Photo
Bringing It All Back Home
Castle in the Village
Everybody Has to Be Somebody
Fallen Angels
Father's Day
Favourite Nights
Finishing Touches
The Gingerbread Lady
God Says There Is No Peter Ott
How the Other Half Loves
The Independent Female
Joe Egg
The Knight at the Twelfth
  Saucer
The Last of the Red Hot Lovers
Norman Conquests
Nuts
Opal is a Diamond
Opal's Husband
Opal's Million Dollar Duck
A Raisin in the Sun
The River
Roads to Home
Safe House
The Sand Castle
Sister Mary Ignatius
Split
String
Tennessee
Trouble in Mind
Two O'Clock Feeding
Victory on Mrs. Dandywine's
  Island

Four Women

Am I Blue?
A Bad Year for Tomatoes
Bedroom Farce
Children of a Lesser God
Clara's Ole Man
A Clearing in the Woods
The Cocktail Party
Crimes of the Heart
The Dark of the Moon and the
  Full
A Delicate Balance
Design for Living
For the Use of the Hall
Going to See the Elephant
I am a Camera
The Lady from Dubuque
Loose Ends
Lovers
The Loves of Cass McGuire
A Matter of Gravity
Opal's Baby
The Primary English Class
Separate Ceremonies
6 Rms Riv Vu
A Touch of Marble
Trevor
Twigs
Wings

Five or More Women

And Miss Reardon Drinks
  a Little
Auntie Mame
The Autumn Garden
Beauty and the Beast
Les Belles Soeurs
Black Girl
Bonjour La Bonjour
Catsplay
The Chalk Garden
Clothes for a Summer Hotel
Confessions of a Female
  Disorder
The Corrupters
Crown Matrimonial
The Curious Savage
The Dancers
First Breeze of Summer
Forty Carats
Funnyhouse of a Negro
Gift of Murder
Golda
Goodbye My Fancy
Hay Fever
Hot L Baltimore
I Just Wanted Someone to Know
Josephine: the Mouse Singer
Killings on the Last Line
The Lark
The Last of Mrs. Lincoln
Lovers
Lovers and Other Strangers
The Madwoman of Chaillot
Major Barbara
A Member of the Wedding
The Miracle Worker
Mornings at Seven
Once a Catholic
A Palm Tree in a Rose Garden
Please, No Flowers
The Prime of Miss Jean Brodie
Reflections in a Window
The Rimers of Eldritch
Roomful of Roses
The Secret Affairs of Mildred
  Wild
Standard Safety
Steaming
Sunset/Sunrise

Two Sides of Darkness
Up the Down Staircase
A Very Rich Woman
Vivat! Vivat! Regina!
A Young Lady of Property

APPENDIX 2:

Directory of Agents
and Publishers

Amber Lane Press
9a Newbridge Road
Ambergate, Derbyshire, DE5 2GR
England

American Place Theater
see   Performing Arts Journal

Lois Berman
250 West 57th Street
New York, N.Y. 10019

Crown Publishers, Inc.
1 Park Avenue
New York, N.Y. 10016

Curtis Brown, Ltd.
1 Craven Hill
London, W2 3EP, England

Bertha Case
42 West 53rd Street
New York, N.Y. 10019

Chatto & Windus, Ltd.
40-42 William IV Street
London, England

Chilton Book Company
Chilton Way
Radnor, PA 19089

Toby Cole: Actors and Authors Agency
234 West 44th Street
New York, N.Y. 10036

The Dramatic Publishing Co.
4150 N. Milwaukee Ave.
Chicago, Ill. 60641

The Dramatists Guild, Inc.
234 West 44th Street
New York, N.Y. 10036

Dramatists Play Service, Inc.
440 Park Ave. South
New York, N.Y. 10016

Elek Books, Ltd.
54-58 Caledonian Road
London, England

Faber and Faber, Ltd.
3 Queen Square
London, England WC1N 3AU

Farrar, Straus, & Giroux
19 Union Square W.
New York, N.Y. 10003

Harold Freedman, Brandt, & Brandt, Inc.
1501 Broadway
New York, N.Y. 10036

Samuel French
25 West 45th Street
New York, N.Y. 10036

Andrew Gellis
Michael Bloom
400 Madison Ave.
New York, N.Y. 10017

John Goodwin
38 Melrose Ave.
Montreal, Quebec, H4A 2S3
Canada

Granada Pub., Ltd.
866 U.N. Plaza
New York, N.Y.

Hill and Wang, Inc.
Dramabooks
72 Fifth Avenue
New York, N.Y. 10011

Michael Imison Playwrights, Ltd.
150 West 47th Street,   Suite 5F
New York, N.Y. 10026

Lester Lewis Associates
156 East 52nd Street
New York, N.Y. 10022

Methuen London, Ltd.
11 New Fetter Lane,
London, EC4P 4EE, England

New American Plays
see Hill and Wang, Inc.

Performing Arts Journal
P.O. Box 858
Peter Stuyvesant Station
New York, N.Y. 10009

Pioneer Drama Service
2176 South Colorado Blvd.
Denver, Colorado 80222

Plays of the Year
see Elek Books, Ltd.

Madeline Puccioni
1272 Donald Drive
Rodeo, Calif. 94572

Ramdom House, Inc.
201 East 50th Street
New York, N.Y. 10022

Susan Rivers
   c/o F. K. Van Patten
Eureka Theater
2299 Market St.
San Francisco, Calif. 94114

Flora Roberts
65 E. 55th St.
New York, N.Y. 10022

Howard Rosenstone
850 7th Avenue
New York, N.Y. 10019

San Francisco Mime Troupe
855 Treat Street
San Francisco. Calif. 94110

Susan   Schulman
165 West End Ave. #28K,
New York, N.Y. 10023

Adele Edling Shank
Dramatic Art Dept.
University of Calif.
Davis, Calif. 95616

Beverly Simons
2540 Bellevue Ave.
West Vancouver, B.C.
Canada

Smyrna Press
Box 1803-GPO
Brooklyn, N.Y.   11202

Talonbooks
201   1019 East Cordova
Vancouver, B.C. V6A 1M8
Canada

University of Queensland Press
St. Lucia
Queensland, Austrailia

Harvey Unna & Stephen Durbridge, Ltd.
24-32 Pottery Lane
Holland Park
London, England

Viking-Penguin, Inc.
625 Madison Ave.
New York, N.Y.   10022

West Coast Plays
P.O. Box 7206,
Berkeley, Calif.   94707

Audrey Wood
Ashley Famous Agency, Inc.
1301 Avenue of the Americas
New York, N.Y.   10019

Bibliography

PLAYS FOR AND ABOUT WOMEN

Barlow, Judith E. ed. Plays by American Women: The Early Years. New York: Bard/ Avon Books, 1981.

France, Rachel, ed. A Century of Plays by American Women. New York: Richards Rosen Press, Inc. 1979.

Hanger, Eunice. 2D and Other Plays. St. Lucia, Queensland, Australia: University of Queensland Press, 1978.

LaTempa, Susan, ed. New Plays By Women. Berkeley, Calif: Shameless Hussy Press, 1979.

Miles, Julia, ed. The Women's Project. New York: Performing Arts Journal Publication, 1980.

Moore, Honor, ed. The New Women's Theater. New York: Vintage Books, div. Random House, 1977.

Sullivan, Victoria, and Hatch, James, eds. Plays By and About Women. New York: Random House, 1973.

Wandor, Michelene, ed. Plays by Women vol. 1. London: Metheun Theatrefile, 1982.

Wandor, Michelene, ed. Plays by Women vol. 2. London: Metheun Theatrefile, 1983.

WORKS ABOUT WOMEN IN THEATER

Cotton, Nancy, ed. Women Playwrights in England, c. 1363-1750. Lewisburg: Bucknell University Press, 1980.

Lenz, Carolyn Ruth Swift; Greene, Gail; and Neely, Carolyn Thomas; eds. The Woman's Part: Feminist Criticism of Shakespeare. Urbana, Ill: The University of Illinois Press, 1980.

Malpede, Karen. Women in Theatre: Compassion and Hope. New York: Drama Book Publishers, 1983.

Olauson, Judith. The American Woman Playwright: A View of Criticism and Characterization. Troy, N.Y.: The Whitston Publishing Company, 1981.

WORKS ABOUT THEATER

Baker's Theatre Bookstore. Baker's Play Catalogue. Boston, Mass. (series).

Ballet, Arthur H. ed. Playwrights for Tomorrow. Minneapolis: University of Minneapolis Press, 1973. (series).

Brasmer, William; Consolo, Dominic, eds. Black Drama: An Anthology. Columbus, Ohio: Charles E. Merrill Publishing Co. 1970.

Burns Mantle Best Plays.   see Guernsey, Otis L. ed. Best Plays series.

Childress, Alice, ed. Black Scenes. Garden City, N.Y.: Doubleday and Company, Inc. 1971.

Corrigan, Robert W. ed. New American Plays vol.1. New York: Hill and Wang, Inc. 1965.

Couch, William Jr. ed. New Black Playwrights. Baton Rouge: Louisiana State University Press, 1968.

Delgado, Ramon, ed. 1982-   . Mayorga, Margaret, ed. 1937-1961, Richards, Stanley, ed. 1968-1981. Best Short Plays. New York: Chilton Book Co.

Dramatists Play Service. Complete Catalogue of Plays. New York: (series).

Foster, Rick, ed. West Coast Plays. Berkeley, Calif.: The California Theater Council. (series) 1977-

French, Samuel, Inc. Samuel French's Basic Catalogue of Plays. New York: (series) 1830-

Guernsey, Otis L. ed. The Best Plays Series (Burns Mantle). New York: Dodd Mead. (series) 1894-

Hatch, James C. ed. Black Theater USA: 45 Plays by Black Americans. New York: The Free Press, div. MacMillan Publishing Co., Inc. 1974.

Hoffman, William, ed. Gay Plays. New York: Avon Books, 1979.

Patterson, Lindsay, ed. Black Theater. New York: New American Library, 1971.

Richards, Stanley, ed. The Best Plays of the Seventies. Garden City, N.Y.: Doubleday, 1980.

Richards, Stanley, ed. The Best Plays of the Sixties. Garden City, N.Y.: Doubleday, 1970.

Richards, Stanley, ed. Best Short Plays of World Theater, 1958-1967. New York: Crown Publishers, 1968.

Stasio, Marilyn, ed. Broadway's Beautiful Losers. New York: Delacorte Press, 1972.

Trewin, J. C. ed. Plays of the Year. London: Paul Elek Ltd. (series) 1949-

Willis, John, ed. Theatre World New York: Crown Publishers, (series) 1949-

WOMEN AND LITERATURE

Fannin, Alice; Luckens, Rebecca; Mann, Catherine Hoyser; eds. Woman: An Affirmation. Lexington, Mass.: D.C. Heath and Company, 1979.

Ferguson, Mary Anne, ed. Images of Women in Literature. Boston, Mass.: Houghton Mifflin, 1973.

Miller, Casey; and Smith, Kate. Words and Women. Garden City, N.Y.: Anchor/Doubleday, 1976.

Index of Playwrights

Index of Characters

Where both surnames and given names are used in the play, the characters are listed twice.

About the Author

SANDRA HEYS, a former drama teacher and community theater director, is a writer and independent producer of audio-visual materials.